Canine Tracking Guide

TRAINING THE ALL-PURPOSE TRACKER

By Don Abney

EDITORIAL

Andrew DePrisco *Editor-in-Chief*
Amy Deputato *Senior Editor*
Jamie Quirk *Editor*

ART

Joanne Muzyka *Senior Graphic Artist*
Bill Jonas *Book Design*
Joanne Muzyka *Digital Imaging*

The publisher would like to thank the following photographers for their contributions to this book:
AnetaPics/Shutterstock, Bernard Brinkmann, Will de Veer, Isabelle Francais, Carol Ann Johnson, Diane
Lewis/AKC Stewart Event Images, Karen Taylor, Michael Trafford, and Alice van Kempen

Original Print ISBN: 978-1-59378-674-8

Library of Congress Cataloging-in-Publication Data

Abney, Don.
  Canine tracking guide / by Don Abney.
      p. cm. — (Country dogs series)
  ISBN 978-1-59378-674-8
  1. Tracking dogs. I. Title.
  SF428.75.A26 2008
  636.7'0886—dc22
                                        2008029187

This book has been published with the intent to provide accurate and authoritative information in regard to the
subject matter within. While every precaution has been taken in the preparation of this book, the author and publisher
expressly disclaim any responsibility for any errors, omissions, or adverse effects arising from the use or application of
the information contained herein. The techniques and suggestions are used at the reader's discretion and are not to be
considered a substitute for veterinary care. If you suspect a medical problem, consult your veterinarian.

i-5 Publishing, LLC™
3 Burroughs, Irvine, CA 92618
www.facebook.com/i5press
www.i5publishing.com

Contents

Introduction

Prior to any training, you should know that your dog already has the ability to smell and track. This is an inherited ability bestowed on every dog at birth. Since the dog is already proficient at this, you are actually going to teach him to identify a specific scent and lead you to its origin.

The information contained within these pages will help teach your dog to track a specific type of game, track a blood trail left behind by wounded game, find a lost person, or identify the presence of any scent, whether you are using your dog for hunting, working, or competition. I have used and taught these methods for search and rescue, tracking, cadaver, narcotics, arson, and game dogs with a great degree of success.

After spending a considerable amount of time studying human scent, I have concluded that all animals have their own individual scent. There is a common scent within each species, but each individual has a complex composition of cells that personalizes his or her scent. This individuality makes it possible for the dog to identify a specific scent and locate the source of that scent.

In training a dog to search for the source of a specific scent, you must realize that he knows the differences in these various scents. Your job is to teach him what and when to track. He can do that—and more—if the proper training is applied.

After reading this book, you may believe that this all sounds too simple. You must maintain your patience when training if you want your dog to understand what it is you are asking him to do. He does not understand human language, and you will have to learn to read the dog's actions and body language to know when he is working and what he is doing. You will have to learn to accept what the dog is trying to tell you and trust his judgment. Once he is taught, you will have a dog that will track almost any scent. It is just a matter of isolating the scent so that he knows what it is you want him to locate.

The greatest problem you will encounter in this training is your acceptance of the fact that the dog knows where the track is and where the scent is coming from. You will inevitably second-guess your dog and have him prove to you that you are mistaken before you come to realize that he knows what he is doing. Accepting this is the hardest thing for any handler to overcome. Following your dog into areas that you believe are incorrect is very hard, but when he shows you the source of the scent, you will become a believer. Dogs do not lie, and to them this is simply a game of hide-and-seek. Your dog is not going to take you out into strange areas just to make you look foolish.

The first dog I trained to track wounded prey was a Louisiana Catahoula Leopard Dog. Using the methods described in this book, I began training her at the age of seven months. In six short weeks, she successfully tracked and located her first wounded deer.

All dogs can detect scent, but some have a nose better suited for scent work and a stronger drive to locate the source of that scent. Shorter noses or the lack of this drive is what deters the use of some breeds for tracking. This book contains guidelines that will help you choose the right dog within a litter. You will have to decide which breed you want to use for the job.

The most legendary nose in dogdom
belongs to the Bloodhound.

The Dog's Nose

Of all the dog's senses, the sense of smell is the most well developed, and the one on which he depends most throughout his life. Puppies are deaf and blind at birth and remain so for the first ten days of life, but they can locate their source of food (mom) within minutes of being delivered. When a birthing female leaves the den or whelping box to relieve herself, eat, or exercise, her puppies instinctively find a corner and bunch up for warmth. The pups know when she returns and can locate her, despite not being able to see or hear, because of their acute sense of smell.

The sense of smell is vital to mature dogs' social skills. It enables them to quickly distinguish between known and unknown humans and other animals. In the male of the species, it is a primary factor in his ability to determine whether a female is in heat and receptive to mating. A dog also can smell certain changes in human body chemistry that influence his behavior. For example, in a state of fear or panic the human body produces adrenaline. Dogs can sense the

A. First sense to develop:
   Dog   Smell
   Human   Touch

B. Primary sense for recognition:
   Dog   Smell
   Human   Sight

C. Last sense to fail:
   Dog   Smell
   Human   Touch/taste

odor of adrenaline—the smell of fear—which provokes reactions ranging from heightened alertness to aggression. Through a combination of instinct and training, a tracking dog will be more motivated and work more intensely when searching for a person who is exhibiting fear.

How Keen Is the Dog's Sense of Smell?

By various calculations over the years, many individuals have estimated that dogs can detect scent ten times better than humans can. In truth, no one knows the exact capacity or efficiency of the dog's nose, because no man-made instrument is capable of measuring it. We can only speculate as to what degree a dog's nose is more sensitive than a human's, but there is evidence that the dog can detect and identify scent better than any instrument devised by humans.

Estimates of efficiency differ for different odors and different breeds. But even though some dogs' ability is better than others', the dog's keen sense of smell is definitely a genetic trait. A 1972 study of German Wirehaired Pointers by G. Geiger, using a sample of 613 males and 573 females, concluded that 46 percent of the breed's tracking ability and 39 percent of its scenting ability are inherited, whether the offspring come from working or nonworking parents.

When the cells of the nose are measured in the area of one square inch, the dog, with one sniff, allows more than 10,000 scents to be distinguished, categorized, and memorized. With that same sniff, the human can distinguish only 4,000 scents.

In Milo Pearsall and Hugo Verbruggen's book *Scent*, the sensitivity of the dog's nose is described as follows: "The dog can smell some odors at as much as one part per trillion (1 in 1,000,000,000,000)." The following example is given:

One of the substances released by human perspiration is butyric acid. If one gram of this chemical (a small drop in the bottom of a teaspoon) were to be spread throughout a ten-story building, a person could smell it at the window only at the moment of release. If this same amount were spread over the entire city of Philadelphia, a dog could smell it anywhere, even up to an altitude of 300 feet.

This example shows that a dog does not suffer from nose fatigue or acclimation to any specific scent. A human, on the other hand, acclimates to the smells around him. When you walk into a florist shop, the combined fragrance of the flowers and plants can be

Another impressive nose is that of the Basset Hound. Taking a hound for a leisurely walk can be a challenge, as the dog always wants to stop and sniff.

overwhelming. It is very difficult for humans to identify and locate any specific scent in this powerful mixture of perfumes. If you were to remain in the shop for a day, however, like those who work there, the powerful smell of fresh flowers would fade, and you would not notice the

The long ears of the scenthound are designed to help gather and hold scent.

aroma as you did when you first walked in. The dog, on the other hand, can smell the individual scents and identify their origins.

The Anatomy of Smell

The ability to detect subtle odors and follow a scent depends on cellular structures called olfactory receptor cells. The olfactory receptor cells are found in the moist lining of the entire length of a dog's nasal cavity. Protruding from the surface of the olfactory cells are hairlike fibers known as cilia. The cilia are believed to be the part of the cell that is stimulated by the molecules of various airborne odors. The dog's nose contains approximately 220 million olfactory cells, with 120 to 200 cilia per cell. By comparison, a human's nose contains approximately 5 million olfactory cells, with six to eight cilia per cell. This would give the dog an estimated olfactory capacity a thousand times greater than that of a human. (By cilia count alone, a human's sense of smell comes closest to that of the frog. A frog's nose contains six to twelve cilia per cell, leading some to conclude that even frogs have a better sense of smell than humans do.)

Mucus membranes in the lining of the dog's nose secrete a thin clear layer of mucus. In addition to its dirt-trapping function, the mucus keeps the olfactory cells moist and helps capture, absorb, and dissolve scent molecules, concentrating them in the cilia as the dog inhales or sniffs. The cilia stimulate the olfactory receptor cells, which are connected by a rich network of olfactory nerves to the olfactory lobe in the dog's brain, where the scent molecules are identified and then categorized in the dog's memory.

The dog also has a secondary olfactory cavity, called the vomeronasal organ (VMO) or Jacobson's organ. This pair of fluid-filled sacs, above the roof of the mouth behind the incisors, is also lined with olfactory receptor cells, but unlike the cells in the nasal cavity, the VMO cells have tiny cellular protuberances instead of cilia that are stimulated by odor molecules. VMO cells transmit impulses directly to the olfactory lobe and, it is believed, to the parts of the dog's brain that are associated with sexual behavior and the detection of pheromones, or chemicals that trigger a natural behavioral response in other animals. The vomeronasal nerve, along which these impulses are carried, may also be stimulated without inhaling, such as when the dog's nose is

submerged in water. The dog's well-developed VMO could explain dogs' superior ability to recognize individual people and other animals by scent.

A third sensory nerve, the trigeminal nerve, lies at the back of the nasal cavity. This nerve sends impulses to the brain to indicate the presence of foreign material within the nasal cavity, which triggers a sneeze. When a dog sneezes or blows his nose, he clears debris that may be interfering with his ability to detect scent, and he distributes additional moisture to the olfactory cells.

Brain anatomy also helps explain why dogs' sense of smell is so much better than humans'. Researchers say the olfactory bulb of the human brain is approximately the size of a pea. A dog's olfactory lobe is up to eight times larger; a bloodhound's olfactory lobe, for example, is about the size of your thumb.

Another anatomical contrast between human and dog involves the capacity of the nasal cavities. The volume of air required to fill the human nose is 1.5 cubic inches; the volume of air required to fill the average dog's nose is 6 cubic inches. The dog therefore has four times as much air swirling over his olfactory receptors. When a dog sniffs, he can hold several bursts of airborne scent molecules in the nasal cavity at once.

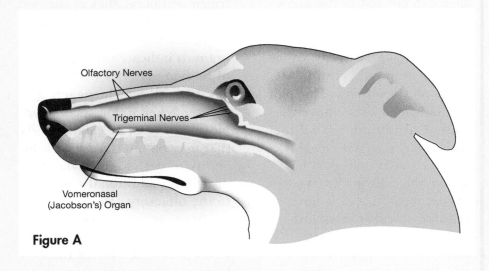

Olfactory Nerves

Trigeminal Nerves

Vomeronasal (Jacobson's) Organ

Figure A

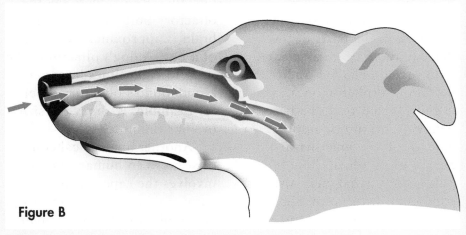

Figure B

The diagram in figure A is a cross-section of the dog's nasal cavity and indicates the locations of the olfactory, trigeminal, and vomeronasal structures.

During the normal breathing cycle (figure B), air is taken in through the nostrils, flows upward, curves approximately midway in the canal, and is directed into the lungs.

During the sniffing cycle (figure C), air is taken forcefully through the nostrils and fills the entire cavity. Sniffing causes air to be pushed against the upper and back walls of the cavity. Inhaled air stays in the nasal passages longer, so more scent molecules can be accumulated and identified. The air then curves and passes into the lungs.

Factors That Affect the Sense of Smell

The more olfactory receptor cells there are, and the greater the nasal capacity, the more olfactory data can be processed by the brain. We would naturally conclude, therefore, that dogs with elongated noses appear to be better suited for scent work. In fact, long-nosed breeds are most often chosen. This is not to say that a short-nosed dog

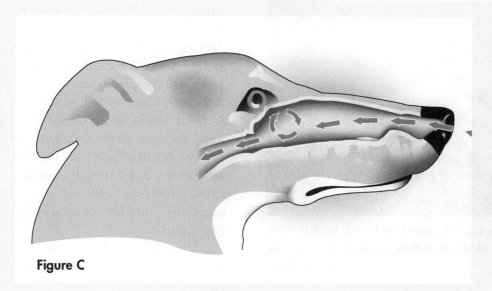

Figure C

With his long muzzle and amply sized nostrils, the German Shepherd Dog is prized for his scenting ability.

Brachycephalic, or short-faced, breeds have the facial structure that is least advantageous for tracking.

cannot do scent work. It is merely to point out that the elongated nose has the advantage of drawing in more scent when sniffing.

Environmental factors also influence a dog's scenting ability. Conditions that cause the dog's nose to dry out can significantly reduce his ability to identify specific scents. Working in hot, dry weather for extended periods is one example. Under such conditions, moisture applied to the outside of the dog's nose will aid in keeping it moist.

Certain diseases can also interfere with the dog's ability to distinguish and identify scent. Among these illnesses are parainfluenza (kennel cough), distemper, rabies, central nervous system disease, hypothyroidism, and Cushing's syndrome. Another cause of the loss of scenting ability is the use of a nasal vaccine. These vaccines, such as Bordetella, which may be administered intranasally, could cause a temporary loss of scenting ability for up to seventy-two hours.

The cells in a dog's nose regenerate on a two-week cycle.

This natural regeneration will help the dog recover from any temporary loss of scenting ability. Cell regeneration is a normal function that occurs without any noticeable or outward signs from the dog.

In spite of the above facts, humans still tend to second-guess a dog when he is leading them down a scent trail and toward the origin of a specific scent. Even today, with dogs' record of tracking success and growing scientific knowledge of the capabilities of the dog's nose, humans will still second-guess the dog. It appears that people just have trouble accepting the fact that the dog's nose is better equipped to locate a trail and reveal its origin more efficiently.than anything else known to man today. Learning to accept what their dog is telling them is the biggest obstacle for dog handlers to overcome in working with tracking dogs. Perhaps, sometime in the future, an instrument will be invented that will outperform the dog, but until then try to accept the fact that the dog's nose knows.

Along with large nostrils and long ears, scenthounds typically have jowls and folds of skin around the head, neck, and chest, also for gathering and holding scent.

Sighthounds tend to have long, narrow muzzles and smaller noses than scenthounds.

Hunters on horseback have traditionally been accompanied by packs of scenthounds—Bloodhounds, Beagles, foxhounds, and so forth—long prized for their superior noses.

Scent

Scent, as defined by the American
Heritage Dictionary, is: (1) a distinctive odor; (2) a
perfume; (3) the trail of a hunted animal or fugitive; or
(4) to detect by smelling. All of these definitions will
apply when describing your dog's actions while in
training or when working.

Just as a fingerprint is unique to an individual, a scent
is a distinctive odor derived from each individual's genetic
material and the chemical activity within his or her body.
With the exception of identical twins living in the same
household, each living creature has a unique individual
scent. It is commonly thought that identical twins carry the
same scent because they developed from the same fertilized
egg, which split during gestation. In recent tests involving
tracking identical twins, however, some dogs could
correctly track and identify the correct subject.

Telltale Scurf
The distribution of scent cannot be controlled. It is a
perfume that cascades from the body and leaves an

invisible indicator of where we are and where we have been. This distinctive odor is distributed by means of sloughing off dead skin cells, known as scurf. Humans shed approximately 10,000 of these dry dead skin cells per second. Although undetectable by the naked eye, these cells create a path that a dog, using his sensitive nose, can follow.

Visualize a lawn mower moving across a lawn. As it cuts, it discharges grass clippings outward along the same path that the mower travels, leaving behind a clear indication of where the mower has been. We can easily see and easily follow the trail. Similarly, scurf cascades from the body, leaving behind a path that the dog identifies and follows when he is tracking.

In Charles Shultz's cartoon *Peanuts*, the character Pigpen provides a great visual example of scurf. Whenever Pigpen appears, a cloud of dust surrounds him. Keep the image of Pigpen in mind when you observe any living animal. Although our own "cloud" is invisible, this is exactly what is taking place every minute of every day. Those microscopic particles that continually cascade off the body would appear as a dust storm if they were visible. It is the unique dust cloud that each of us leaves behind that enables the dog to recognize the specific scent of a person, or an item that has been handled by that person. Whether animal or human, we all leave behind a mapped trail, generally undetectable by humans, but a mere sniff away for canines.

A demonstration by the Association of Louisiana Deputy Sheriffs showed the ability of the dog to detect a specific minute scent and follow it. Sheriffs from all of the state's parishes (counties) attended the demonstration. With the assembly gathered in a hotel parking lot, one sheriff volunteer was asked to select a blank round from a bag of 100 blanks and load that round into a gun he did not own. He was instructed to fire the blank and to eject it without ever touching it again. Once the spent shell casing was expelled, he was told to create a trail and find a hiding place.

He left the parking lot of the hotel and crossed into a field.

About fifty yards into the field, he circled a storage trailer and then returned to the hotel. There he climbed an exterior stairway to a second-floor balcony and hid in a doorway from which he could view the proceeding below. A dog was brought to the area where the spent round lay on the ground and was readied for the search. The casing was picked up using an ink pen, so as not to contaminate it by touch, and presented to the dog. After sniffing the casing, the dog was given a command to begin the search and was released. The dog traveled the same path that the sheriff had walked and located the subject on the second-floor balcony in full view of all in attendance. The total elapsed time of the search, from the dog's release to finding the subject, was less than one minute and covered an area of approximately 300 yards.

How much scent is needed to perform a search? Tests performed by the National Aeronautics and Space Administration (NASA) showed that an astronaut in an encapsulated spacesuit with only his face exposed could still be detected by

Sniffing certain areas of the body lets dogs learn a lot about each other.

a canine. The simple presence of a person or other animal leaves behind enough scent to be detected by a dog.

Scent Glands

Most animals have a scent-producing gland used for marking territory and attracting the opposite sex. The following list identifies some of the animals that are known to have scent glands and where those glands are located. This list will prove to be a valuable resource in training your tracking dog. Knowing where the majority of scent indicators are located and utilizing those parts facilitates the training process.

1. Dog and skunk: anal area
2. Fox: tail and feet
3. Deer, antelope, moose: legs and hooves
4. Boar: back, along the ridge
5. Bear: anal area and alongside hair follicles
6. Squirrel: lateral body wall
7. Opossum, raccoon: breast
8. Rabbit: facial area

It is unknown whether humans possess scent glands analogous to those of other species. There is some belief that humans produce pheromones that influence behavior—for example, that the release of certain hormones during a woman's menstrual cycle affects physical attraction in males—but to date no scientific study has proved or disproved this theory.

Scent Patterns

Scent trails take three distinct forms, all of which dogs utilize in locating the source of scent. These patterns are known as cone, trapped, and scattered. You should familiarize yourself with all three patterns and the conditions that create them; all may be encountered in any given area,

and with familiarity you will be better able to lend assistance to your dog.

The cone formation develops under ideal weather conditions. In this case, scent spreads outward and upward from the point of origin in a manner best represented by a horizontal ice cream cone. This pattern best develops when there is only a slight breeze. It is the easiest pattern for a dog to work because the intensity of the scent gradually becomes stronger as the dog moves closer to the source and weaker as he moves away from it. Your dog will move faster and more diligently as the scent cone narrows, and he will indicate to the handler that he is nearing the scent source.

Scent can become trapped, or pooled, in an area and fail to form the natural cone pattern. The trapped pattern often occurs in uneven, hilly, mountainous terrain or areas containing thick shrubbery or undergrowth. Wind conditions will force scent downward and horizontally, causing it to circulate around these obstructions and become trapped behind them. This is very similar to the manner in which water passes around an object, causing an eddy to form on the downstream side of the object.

Scent also can be trapped in low, dish-shaped areas and behind barriers protected from the wind, which creates a small scent pool. Hilly, sloping, or mountainous terrain is difficult to work because of its shape alone, but trapped scent can make the dog's job more difficult. When scent is trapped or pooled, the dog will linger in one place, drawn by the amount of scent held in the area. Depending on the amount of scent present in the pool, he may react in a frantic confused manner or give a partial indication of locating the source and suddenly begin searching the same area again. He may circle the same area over again in an attempt to locate the source. It now becomes the handler's responsibility to assist the dog in moving away from the pool and locating the path taken.

To accomplish this, the handler must lead the dog away from the object and begin working in a widening circular pattern away from the pool until the dog recognizes the scent path and begins tracking again. Be patient; the dog will want to return to the pooled location because of the strength of scent in the pool. You must continue working him away from the pool until he is back on track.

Scent is considered scattered when a moderate wind prevents the formation of a cone and casts scent over a wider area. Wind has its greatest effect on scent in open fields. Strong winds can create a variety of other problems, blowing away the scent and causing it to accumulate in areas that could be misleading. When scattered, scent will hold to the areas of resistance, such as the edge of the woods running alongside an open field. In this situation, it becomes the handler's responsibility to assist the dog in maintaining a course of direction to follow. Direction is determined by the probable direction of travel and the lay of the land. This proves to be the most difficult situation in which to identify a track, and experience in these situations will be the most valuable guide. Fortunately, most dogs will figure out this problem on their own, but handlers must know when their dogs are in need of assistance.

Conditions That Enhance or Degrade Scent Trails

Wind is not the only influence on scent pattern formation. People, animals, and weather conditions can have a direct effect on scent by causing contamination, dilution, destruction, and displacement of a scent trail. People and animals can disrupt and contaminate scent trails by walking across them or wandering around on the trail. The greater the number, the more contaminated it becomes, increasing the difficulty for dogs to detect the correct scent and direction of travel. Whenever possible, keep the scent trail as sterile as possible. There are times when it is necessary for more people to enter an area, but try to control the numbers as much as possible. The dog has the ability to identify that one scent, but the more scents there are, the more difficult his job becomes. Remember, the easier it is for him to do his job, the faster a recovery is made.

Rain, sun, and humidity are also known to disperse, dilute, disrupt, and destroy scent. Rain can have a positive or a negative effect on scent by either reinforcing or cleansing the trail.

A light rainfall will force scent to the ground and hold it in place, and when the rain stops, the process of evaporation will regenerate the scent, causing it to rise again. Dew and humidity have a similar enhancing effect on scent, keeping it close to the ground and making it easier for the dog to follow the trail. This is one reason why early morning and late evening searches are more productive and yield more successful recoveries than do searches at other times of day.

Heavy rainfall and thunderstorms can dilute, displace, or destroy scent trails, depending on the volume and duration of rainfall. The rule of thumb is that when a thunderstorm continues for two hours or more, there is little likelihood of an intact scent trail. If the rainfall is less than an hour in length, the scent trail may be unaffected. Even though rainfall could have a washing effect on a scent trail, do not abandon the search. You never know where the scent may be or if your dog can detect it. Continue your efforts until you are completely sure that you have exhausted all possibilities.

Sunlight is perhaps the biggest enemy of scent. Depending on cloud cover and the intensity of the sun, ultraviolet rays can destroy the presence of a scent trail in a matter of hours. Aged tracks are more difficult to follow in open fields due to the effects of sun and wind. You will become aware of this as you observe your dog performing a zigzag, or serpentine, pattern when working in an open field. The serpentine pattern may be wide or narrow, but the dog will move from side to side trying to locate the scent and pinpoint the trail. It should be noted at this point that scent will migrate into cooler areas as if to deliberately avoid destruction. In an open field, therefore, your dog may move into shady areas instead of working directly on the trail.

Since scent will seek a cooler area, never abandon a track because of streams, lakes, or ponds. What you are looking for may be located in them, and your dog can detect that. We have documented dogs traveling from point to point over land and water to locate a missing person.

Certain environmental factors can degrade a scent, making the dog work harder to stay on trail.

No matter how difficult or aimless a search may appear to you, let the dog be your guide. He is better equipped to determine the presence of scent and follow a scent trail.

Carbon monoxide from vehicles could contaminate a trail and hamper a dog's ability to identify a scent. Whenever possible, locate and direct exhaust fumes behind the dog. This is not to say that a dog cannot work effectively in close proximity to carbon monoxide exhaust. In one documented case, a Bloodhound tracked a one-day-old human trail made by a person inside a moving automobile. The dog tracked the person's scent along a highway for a number of miles to locate the victim.

With their scenting ability and high tractability, retriever breeds
are often trained and used for search-and-rescue work.

Selecting a Tracking Dog

Any breed can be taught tracking work, but medium-built breeds with elongated noses are most highly recommended. The larger breeds tend to be more cumbersome, suffer more injuries, and tire very rapidly, which means they cannot sustain long hours of work.

Consider Breed Characteristics

Begin breed selection by eliminating pug-nosed dogs. Because of their shorter noses, they have a diminished capacity for doing scent work. Breeds with longer noses have little difficulty identifying and retaining the scent much longer. You will have more success with breeds that come from the hunting, working, or herding classes than you will with dogs that have shorter or blunt noses. Any dog with an elongated nose is capable of performing the tasks described in this book.

Take your time when selecting the breed that you would like to use. Investigate all the pros and cons of the breed you're interested in prior to making a decision. The

Along with an elongated muzzle and medium build in adulthood, the main criterion for choosing a future tracker is to pick a pup with whom you'll enjoy working.

physical problems that would hamper their success in the field. If you are looking for a breed of dog that will not cause you any inconvenience, you can stop right here. The only dogs that fit the category of never being sick, injured, or in need of care are made of concrete or plastic. Try as you might, those dogs will never do the job of tracking.

If the dog you choose is to be a family dog as well as a working dog, then discuss the various breeds with your family. They will have to live with the dog as well, and they should have some input into which breeds would fit into the family.

Compare Puppies Within a Litter

When selecting a dog for tracking work, selecting the right dog from within a litter of puppies is just as important as breed selection. Not all puppies will work or display the drive of the parents. Contrary to popular thought, breeding two working dogs together is not necessarily going to produce a litter of working dogs. Breeding two working dogs increases the chance that some of their

particular breed that you choose should be one that appeals to you in temperament as well as in looks. You're looking for a dog that works, but you will be in contact with this dog every day, whether he is in training, working, or just being your buddy, so you should choose a breed that you will enjoy being around.

Every breed has some trait that you might not be fond of; factor this in when making your decision. Some breeds have a tendency to be barkers or diggers. Some shed more than others do. Others are susceptible to eye problems or other offspring will inherit their most desirable traits, but if it were that easy to produce good working dogs, we would not have as many breeds or numbers of dogs that we have today.

Considering genetic influences, bloodlines, and certain other factors, you can obtain working dogs from nonworking parents. By researching the background of the breeding pair, you may find that previous generations in this breeding line were working dogs. This is a positive indicator that the dog you choose will be capable of performing the work desired.

Breeders of working dogs will try to keep the working genes alive in their lines by using only working breeding lines in their breeding program. It is these genes that make up the complete working dog, and that is what makes the dog capable of doing his job. Ask the breeder if the dogs he is breeding come

You're more likely to find working lines in breeds like the scenthounds and German Shepherd, but it's not necessary for your future tracker to come from working parents.

Although it's hard to predict how a mixed-breed pup will mature, mixed-breed dogs have the same potential for training and learning as purebreds.

litters and narrowing down your choice of pup. Set aside time for this important process. Do not set out to view a litter of pups if you are in a rush or have other appointments for that day. It is going to take some time to observe the pups and perform a few tests within the litter. You may find that you need to view a number of litters before you make your decision. Compare it with the process of buying a new car: you would not want to be rushed through the sale. You would want to see the options, prices, colors, and make sure the car fits your driving needs. This decision-making process is just as worthwhile in selecting a tracking dog. You are going to have this dog for a number of years, probably longer than that car, so be patient and pick the right one. Do not settle for something you do not really want thinking that you can change the dog. Do not let the inconvenience or tedium of having to view more puppies lead you to accept any dog. You will only end up resenting the dog and wishing to be rid of him.

from working lines. If the breeder has not kept the working abilities active in his breeding program, I suggest you seek to purchase your puppy from a different breeder.

With that in mind, you are now ready to begin looking at

Purebred or Mixed Breed?

Purebred dogs are those with a known pedigree. Most purebred dogs are part of a lineage of dogs that have been bred for specific traits that are especially useful for specific purposes, such as working, herding, hunting, conformation, and guarding. A great amount of study and testing has gone into creating breeds that are best suited for these activities as well as pleasing to the eye.

When buying a purebred dog, you will likely pay a premium for the time spent testing the dogs to choose the best pair to be bred, caring for the pups after they are born, and nurturing and socializing them until they are ready to leave the litter. Breeding in this manner gives you, the buyer, more trust in the genetic qualifications, health, and temperament of the puppy and more confidence in the dog's eventual ability. You

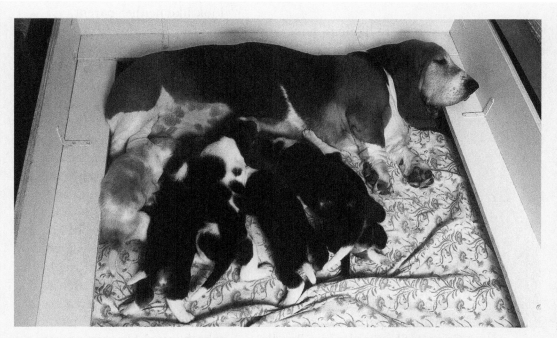

When acquiring any purebred puppy, a reputable breeder is the most reliable source.

Alert and intelligent, Catahoula Leopard Dogs are good choices for many types of working pursuits.

are also more likely to have some recourse if there are any problems with the dog.

Mixed-breed dogs do well in today's society and environment. The only uncertainty in regard to mixed breeds is genetic. The genetic traits that have been inherited from the dog's parents are unknown to you, and you'll have no way of determining which traits are dominant over the others. In other words, the dog's ultimate development is a guess. For example, if you were to acquire a mixed-breed dog knowing its parents were a German Shepherd and a Poodle,

you still would not know what the temperament or attitude of this dog was going to be. Just because he looks like a Shepherd does not mean he will act like one. Of course, all purebred dogs were mixed breeds at one time, but it was breeders' continuous outcropping of genetic differences that produced reliability in the breed. With a mixed-breed litter, you cannot tell which is which. Some may look like Poodles, others may look like Shepherds, while others may look like neither parent.

To some, this explanation may sound biased, but I am a breeder who takes the time to place all of my puppies before any breeding takes place. I have owned and trained mixed-breed dogs with much success. I believe the early training nipped any problems in the bud, but that was because of training and not because of pedigrees or mixed breeding. As a matter of fact, my first dog as a child was a wild puppy that my father caught in the woods. A veterinarian said the dog may have been a cross between a Collie and Spitz, but who knows? He was a great dog! My dad took the time to teach the dog proper manners as soon as he came into the house. Dad did the same with his children, and I came to appreciate this early training.

Male or Female?

Another question that is always part of tracking dog selection is: which sex works better, male or female? A male tends to ride a rollercoaster of hormone imbalances. One day he is at the top of the hill, and the next day he is at the bottom with continuous peaks and valleys. These hormonal swings can change the personality of the dog and lead to some confusion on the part of the owner. Marking his territory and anything else he believes is his can become a problem. Marking can be curtailed with training, but it can also be very nerve-racking. Intact males tend to fight more than do neutered males. Fighting, however, cannot always be blamed on a strong-willed dog wanting to be the leader; sometimes it is the fault of an owner who has been negligent in socializing the dog.

In general, females tend to have a more balanced temperament than males do, but females can be equally troublesome when they come into heat, every six months. In addition to the bleeding that comes with their cycle, they too can exhibit bad attitudes at this time. When she is in the peak of her heat cycle, there is only one thing that she wants, and that is to breed. A working female in heat will need to be pulled from service, as estrus may affect the quality of her work, for a minimum of twenty-one days, twice a year.

Don't pick based on looks alone! Simple personality tests can indicate which pup or pups in a litter show the most promise for certain types of training.

If you spay your female, you will reduce the problems associated with a female dramatically. Neutering a male may produce similar results, but there is no guarantee. If you do not intend to breed your dog, neutering or spaying is well advised, as it will help prevent future medical problems in the reproductive systems. Intact males that are not used for breeding could develop testicular cancer. Intact females can acquire pyometra, a serious uterine infection. These diseases are not what you want to see in animals that you work with and love.

This discussion does not answer the question as to which selection is better, but it gives you an idea of what to expect. The ultimate decision lies with you. You and your family are the ones who will have to deal with the dog, so keep uppermost in your mind the purpose for which you are choosing him.

Evaluating Puppies

You have arrived at the home of the breeder, and you are ready to view the litter. Stop! First you will want to view the breeding pair or at least the dam, if the sire is not on the premises. Viewing the adults will be an indicator of what your grown pup will look like and the type of care the dogs and the puppies have received. Observe the living conditions of the dogs. Are they clean? Are there any foul smells? A nursing bitch may have an odor about her because of the puppies' walking all over her, but she and the puppies are the only exceptions. Do not make excuses because you think the puppies are cute or because the price is a real bargain. All puppies are cute, but what appears as a bargain now may put you in the poorhouse later. Ask important questions about the breeder's guarantees, return policies, problems you should be aware of, and why these two dogs were chosen for breeding.

Now it is time to pick a puppy. I cannot tell you which puppy to pick, but I can help you make a good decision. On pages 34–36, you will find two charts that I use to determine the type, temperament, and working drive of puppies. If you follow the instructions as closely as possible, they may help you decide which puppy to bring home. These charts may be helpful in selecting a grown dog, too, but a few tests, such as picking him up off the ground, may require a little more strength and balance on your part.

The charts are divided into five sections. Each section contains an action to be performed by you and a range of responses or reactions, one of which you will circle for each puppy. There are columns for eight puppies. If you are viewing a litter that has more than eight, evaluate extra puppies on the back of your paper.

Circle the letter corresponding to the response/reaction of every puppy in each section. When you finish each list, count the number of As, Bs, Cs, and Ds for each puppy. At the end of the chart is a score box to enter the total of each letter for each pup. When you have tested all puppies and completed both charts, add the scores for both lists to get a total "grade." If two puppies have an equal grade, the test should be redone for those particular puppies.

Dogs that register a higher number of As would fall into the dominant category and will generally be the leaders. Dogs that fall into this category will make good dogs, but you must take charge of them. This can be a desirable trait if the dog is to be used for guarding or personal protection. Care should be taken around small children until the dog has been trained. Because of the child's smaller stature, the dog will attempt to achieve a dominant position over the child and assume his rightful place in the pecking order. Dogs from this category are often misunderstood. They are chosen because of their outward personality, but when they demonstrate the leadership role, owners often become irritated with what they see as defiance and want to reprimand them. In a pack, the dominant dog is the leader. You must teach your dog that you are the leader and that his position is a lower one, especially around children.

Dogs with mostly Bs and Cs are less dominant. Those in the B range are the ones that I like the best. They are what I refer

GROUP — Observe the entire litter as a group.	1	2	3	4	5	6	7	8
Aggressive. Chases, bites, or downs other puppies.	A	A	A	A	A	A	A	A
Alert to movement or people. Runs toward them.	B	B	B	B	B	B	B	B
Aware of movement or people. Usually the follower.	C	C	C	C	C	C	C	C
Unaware. Stays alone away from the group.	D	D	D	D	D	D	D	D

WALK AWAY — Call puppies. As puppies begin to move, walk away.								
Follows or comes toward the sound.	A	A	A	A	A	A	A	A
Hears sound. Cannot determine direction of sound.	B	B	B	B	B	B	B	B
Looks around but does not move.	C	C	C	C	C	C	C	C
No response.	D	D	D	D	D	D	D	D

LOUD NOISE — (Individual test) Hit pot with large spoon or blow a whistle.								
Startled, but remains in the area.	A	A	A	A	A	A	A	A
Runs away, but returns to area.	B	B	B	B	B	B	B	B
Runs away, but returns cautiously when called.	C	C	C	C	C	C	C	C
Runs away, hides, and will not return when called.	D	D	D	D	D	D	D	D

PLAY DRIVE — (Individual test) Swing a tennis ball on a string close to the puppy.								
Plays with ball grasping it in mouth and tugging.	A	A	A	A	A	A	A	A
Plays with ball, mouths and paws at ball.	B	B	B	B	B	B	B	B
Paws at ball and walks away.	C	C	C	C	C	C	C	C
Sniffs and walks away or ignores ball completely.	D	D	D	D	D	D	D	D

RETRIEVE DRIVE — (Individual test) Roll a tennis ball away from puppy.								
Chases ball, picks it up, and runs away with it.	A	A	A	A	A	A	A	A
Chases ball, plays with it, but does not run off.	B	B	B	B	B	B	B	B
Chases ball, then walks away.	C	C	C	C	C	C	C	C
Does not chase ball or ignores ball completely.	D	D	D	D	D	D	D	D

SOCIAL ATTRACTION — (Individuals) Remove from litter and call puppy to you.	1	2	3	4	5	6	7	8
Runs to you, tail up, jumping, biting at hands.	A	A	A	A	A	A	A	A
Runs to you, tail up, paws at hands.	B	B	B	B	B	B	B	B
Runs to you, tail down, rolls over.	C	C	C	C	C	C	C	C
Does not come.	D	D	D	D	D	D	D	D

PETTING — (Individuals)(Do not restrain) Pet from head to tail. Test for 30 seconds.								
Jumps, paws, and bites at hands.	A	A	A	A	A	A	A	A
Jumps and paws, licks at hands.	B	B	B	B	B	B	B	B
Rolls over and licks at hands.	C	C	C	C	C	C	C	C
Goes away and will not come back.	D	D	D	D	D	D	D	D

FOLLOW — (Individuals) With pup standing next to you, walk away.								
Follows, tail up, runs underfoot, bites at feet.	A	A	A	A	A	A	A	A
Follows, tail up and running underfoot.	B	B	B	B	B	B	B	B
Follows with coaching.	C	C	C	C	C	C	C	C
Does not follow or walks away.	D	D	D	D	D	D	D	D

RESTRAINT — (Individuals) Roll pup on his back and hold down for 30 seconds.								
Fights and bites at hand.	A	A	A	A	A	A	A	A
Fights but does not bite.	B	B	B	B	B	B	B	B
Fights momentarily. May lick at hand.	C	C	C	C	C	C	C	C
Does not fight or lick. Leaves after contact.	D	D	D	D	D	D	D	D

ELEVATION — (Individuals) Pick up from middle of body. Do not squeeze. Hold feet off ground for 30 seconds.								
Fights to get down, growls, or bites at hands.	A	A	A	A	A	A	A	A
Fights momentarily then settles down, licks at hands.	B	B	B	B	B	B	B	B
Fights to get down, no growling or biting.	C	C	C	C	C	C	C	C
Does not struggle, may lick at hands.	D	D	D	D	D	D	D	D

Score

A = DOMINANT	TOTAL							
B = ASSERTIVE	TOTAL							
C = RECEPTIVE	TOTAL							
D = SUBMISSIVE	TOTAL							

to as assertive dogs. In other words, these dogs will not present a dominant posture, but they will not back down if confronted. I find these dogs to be the best for hunting and working. This type of dog will bark a warning, but will not readily bite. Those in the C range may change to the B range once separated from the litter. However, do not take any dog hoping that it will change. Accept what the test and the breeder tells you, and be ready to deal with these traits.

The dogs with mostly Ds are usually very shy dogs. They will approach you in a submissive posture: head down, ears back, tail wagging nervously, with a semi walking/crawling gait. They may urinate and roll over on their backs when approached, or they may do all of the above. Shy dogs tend to be very fearful of anything that is new to them, and they require a great deal of work and socialization. They will make good family pets if you are prepared to spend the time training them. They cannot be forced into new situations but must be allowed to work them out for themselves. Do not expect too much too soon from these dogs.

The sections Loud Noise, Play Drive, and Retrieve Drive on the first selection sheet are important tests if you are look- ing for a working dog. These three tests will help you deter- mine which of the puppies may be better suited for working or hunting.

There are no guarantees that by using these tests you

will get the perfect dog. I have been working with dogs for years, and I can assure you that the perfect dog comes along only occasionally. These tests may assist you in making your decision, but other circumstances could change the outcome after your selection. One is the amount of attention the dog receives. Dogs are pack animals, and they rely on their packs for comfort, safety, and assurance. Your role is pack leader, and it is up to you to set the rules and guidelines for your new addition. Other circumstances are the amount of training, socialization, and exercise your dog will receive. All of these things play a part in the dog's understanding of his place in your family and the quality of work he performs. You must make the commitment to give some of your time to your dog each day.

As my mentor told me, "Never say what your dog or child won't do; they'll make a liar out of you every time." Always use caution when introducing a new pup or dog into your family or new

Scenting comes naturally to all puppies, who use their sense of smell when learning their house-training routines.

surroundings. Be on guard for how the dog will react, especially if he is a grown dog. You really do not know what this dog has been through, and he will need time to adjust to his new family (pack). Do not rush the dog into training as soon as you get him home. Give him some time to adjust to the new lifestyle, smells, environment, and people. After about two weeks of adjustment, you may begin training at a slow, methodical pace.

Finding articles with the person's scent along the
way means that the dog is on the right track.

Scent: Sources, Handling, and Storing

It is always best to use an individual as your tracklayer when you begin to teach your dog tracking. I suggest using assistants whenever possible, because a dog is inspired to perform well when he locates a person who gives him immediate praise and reward. It may not always be convenient, however, for a person to be available when you want to work. The following methods of collecting scent will enable you to work with your dog when no one is available.

Acquiring Scent: Source and Selection

HUMAN

In your quest to acquire human scent, you may get some strange looks from people when you ask them to provide you with scent. It is always best to explain your training involvement first, then ask about obtaining scent. By informing them of what you are doing and the purpose of acquiring their scent, they will be more likely to assist you.

The best source of adult scent is from articles that are worn close to the body and have not been washed, such as a hat, T-shirt, or underwear. Since scurf cascades off the body, the head is a perfect place for transmission. When a hat is worn, it collects scurf in the material, and the sweatband will collect perspiration that contains butyric acid (scent). Underwear that covers the groin area collects a great portion of expelled scent, including some perspiration. Bed clothing is also a good source of scent.

Children's scent is best acquired from articles that have been worn around the neck or a recently used pillowcase. Hats worn by children may be utilized, but be certain that the hat belongs to a particular child

Shoes are not the best articles to use for scent, but dogs seem to like them anyway.

and is not borrowed from someone else. The combination of scents could be misleading and confuse your dog. Shoes and socks are not good scent articles, because of the possible development of mold or fungus that will interfere with the desired scent.

The method I use for collecting scent is to have an individual place four or five gauze or make-up pads inside the waistband of their clothing and touching their skin. Leave the pads in place for approximately twenty minutes. When you are ready to retrieve them, have the person remove them and place them in a sealable plastic bag. If the person is unavailable to work with you and your dog, you have their scent. Simply take out one of the pads and drag it to make your scent trail. Use the bag as your scent indicator; that is, allow the dog to sniff the bag and track to the gauze. Continue using them one at a time until they are all used up. If you are using children for scent gathering, have them wipe their necks with a few pads in

Hides can be used to teach a dog to track animals.

addition to wearing the pads around the waist.

ANIMAL

Acquiring animal scent is simply a matter of acquiring parts of the kind of animal that you wish to locate and using them to lay your trail. Animal hides work as well, but do not salt the hide that you are going to use for laying tracks. If you do not want to cut or use your hide, place some gauze or make-up pads in a sealed container or plastic bag along with the hide or portion of animal you have selected. Allow them to remain in the sealed bag for a minimum of twenty-four hours. Instead of

A successful find. Hides or parts of the animal that you want your dog to track are used to lay a trail.

square, fur side out, and tie it with some string. Place the rolls into sealable plastic bags and store them in a freezer. When you are ready to train, simply remove one of the rolls.

BLOOD

Within the body or extracted into a syringe, blood does not contain any human or animal scent. Blood has an odor, but that odor is iron cells within the blood. Blood is on the inside of a body, and an individual's scent (scurf) is on the outside. Therefore, not until blood is exposed to the exterior of the skin will it collect and hold that individual's scent. If you intend to work blood trails, then you should save fresh blood from the type of animal you want to track.

Collecting blood is not an easy task, and the animal from which you are collecting will have that individual's scent. This is not a major concern, as you will see when you begin using the blood and hides that you have saved. The blood that you collect should be refrigerated but not frozen.

using your hide, take the pads out as they are needed and discard them when work is completed.

If you prefer using the hide, as I do, cut the hide into eight- or ten-inch squares. Roll up each

Handling Scent

It is best to handle your scent article with unpowdered surgical gloves. This eliminates the possibility of another scent being added to your pad or article, and it reduces the amount of your scent coming into direct contact with the article. It will also protect you from contact with any foreign bacteria.

When using a complete article, such as a shirt or a portion of an animal that will not fit in a sealable bag, use a plastic grocery bag. Turn the bag inside out, place your hand inside the bag, and pick up the article using the bag as your glove. Next, turn the bag right side out while holding the article. In this manner, you have not made contact with the article, and you have not contaminated the article with your scent. Tie the handles of the bag together and freeze it.

When using a scent article that has been kept in a freezer, remove the article and allow it to thaw inside its bag at room temperature for a minimum of fifteen minutes prior to use. The time allowed for thawing will rejuvenate the scent inside the plastic bag.

Storing Scent

Refrigeration and freezing are the best methods of storing scent. Place your articles in sealable plastic bags, and store them so they are not touching the wall of the refrigerator or freezer. If you are not going to use your entire supply at one time, separate and place them in individual freezer bags prior to freezing. This method will allow you to remove only what you need for each training session.

When storing blood to be used for working the trail of a wounded animal, do not freeze the blood. When blood is frozen, ice crystals will form inside the container that may affect the blood when thawed. Instead, place it in an airtight container and refrigerate. Use a syringe to remove only the amount of blood that you will require for each outing. Exposure to light, air, and heat will destroy the blood and render it unusable. If the blood begins to turn a dark brown color or has a strong dead odor, it should be discarded.

Once real tracking begins, the dog will be working
on all types of terrain and in all types of cover.

Training Preliminaries

The following chapters on teaching
your dog to track will guide you through the procedures
for training. Bear in mind that your dog will not learn
everything in one session, but he will retain a little more
with each complete training session. This is why it is so
important to conduct each lesson for the full recommended period before advancing to the next lesson.
Although it may appear that he is doing well and understands the lesson, it is always better to reinforce what he
has learned than to cut a lesson short.

When to Train and When Not to Train

The question most often asked is, At what age can
you start teaching a dog to track? A dog may start
training at any age; however, I find it best to begin
training between sixteen weeks and two years of age.
Dogs are capable of beginning training earlier, but
waiting until the series of vaccinations and boosters is
completed is advisable. Most vaccination series are
completed by sixteen weeks of age, providing the dog

the protection he needs against disease.

There are two periods in a dog's life when stress, anxiety, fear, and trauma should be avoided. The first is the Fear Imprint Cycle, which occurs between eight and ten weeks of age. This is the most crucial period in a dog's life. Any trauma experienced by a puppy at this age could have a lifelong effect. By "trauma," I mean from the perspective of the puppy. What we consider to be trauma may not be interpreted the same by the puppy. It is always best to curtail any training or corrections for a puppy at this age. Allowing the puppy to get through this period will be worth more to you in the future than the two weeks of training time you may have lost.

The second period occurs at approximately ten months of age. This period is not as critical as the first, but repeated situations that cause fear could result in a dog that will not respond in an expected manner. For example, if the dog is repeatedly placed in situations that he considers fearful or stressful, he could, without proper exposure or training, become fearful of every situation that was similar in nature. Timing is everything in training, and taking your time when training will be most valuable.

Dogs over two years of age can be trained, but bad habits that have developed over time will have to be broken. Breaking bad habits is a more difficult process and will require more patience and time than teaching him anything new will.

The Training Schedule

During training, a lesson should not be repeated more than three times a session. The dog will view these lessons as a game that he is willing to play, and as he plays he learns the lesson. As long as he views these lessons as a game, he will continue to perform. If a lesson is repeated more than three times a session, he may tire of the game and not want to play. Just as you will limit the number of repetitions in a session, you should limit the number of days of training.

Some trainers believe a dog should be worked every day or he will forget the exercise. I do not subscribe to that theory. By continuously training every day, the dog becomes bored with the game and eventually reaches a learning plateau when he will refuse to do the simplest of things that he did willingly in the past. Your dog does not need to be worked every day, and he will not forget the lesson within a few of days of not being worked. Give him one or two days off during each training week, and he will come back to the lessons willingly and will be excited about the "game" of tracking.

Make an effort to train your dog in a variety of places and surroundings instead of just one location. Changing locations also prevents your dog from working by memory. A dog that is repeatedly worked in the same area will learn where you have hidden the scent and will begin checking each of the locations where your tracklayer or hide was placed before he begins to

actually search for it. By changing sites, he will have to use his nose to locate the scent source. Search areas may be used again, but they should not be used more than once every two to three weeks.

If you are a hunter, do not train your dog in the same area where you intend to hunt. Training him in the same area could, again, have him memory searching. It is OK to use him in the same area when searching for wounded animals, as he will be performing his job.

During the hunting season, if the dog does not have to locate wounded prey, you should play hide-and-seek with him to keep him sharp. During the off-season, the dog should be worked at least once a week to keep him active and interested in the game. Approximately three weeks prior to the hunting season, begin working your dog three times each week. When the season opens, he will be ready to go to work.

Informal Training

It is advisable to work with an assistant whenever possible, but there are times when you may have to work with the dog by yourself. If your training is interrupted while you wait for an assistant to become available, or if you are simply taking a day off from the normal training regimen, here are some informal training techniques you can enjoy with your dog.

Playing fetch with your dog is a fun activity that can be beneficial to your dog's tracking. After all, tracking is just a game of fetch at longer distances, so providing him with a shorter version of the same game will encourage him to work more efficiently at tracking, especially if there is a reward waiting for him.

Here is something to keep in mind: the majority of owners attempt to play fetch by throwing the ball or toy too far before the dog understands the game. Start with short throws of no more than twenty feet. Allow the dog to go to the object and retrieve it on his own. If he is not interested in the game on his own, you will have to teach him. This is not

hard and it does not take long to teach. (You will find instructions on training the dog to fetch in the next section.)

If your dog shows an affinity for playing fetch, you can provide a lot of informal training that will benefit him in performing his job. Play fetch using his favorite toy or a tennis ball. I recommend the tennis ball because it can retain scent, helps the dog identify a specific item, and gives him the incentive to recover it. Open the tennis ball container and allow it to air out until the manufacturer's smell is gone. Place all of the aired-out balls in a can that contains the scent that you wish to work. Keep the container closed for approximately three days, and allow the balls to absorb the scent. Use them one at a time. To aid you in rotating which balls you use, place a number on each of them with a felt-tipped marker.

The dog's saliva will become one of the scents associated with the ball, so you must change the ball with each session. You may reuse a ball after it has been cleaned and rescented. You can clean the balls with a solution of two tablespoons of baking soda in one quart of water. Allow the ball to air dry before placing it back in the can.

Another method of fetch is performed by cutting a length of half-inch-diameter PVC pipe approximately eight inches long. Drill holes all along its length to allow scents to escape. Place your scent article (acquired on a makeup pad) inside the tube, and close it off with end caps. Do not glue the end caps, as you will have to change the scent pad from time to time. As your dog fetches the tube, he will be exposed to the aroma of the scent and begin to key on it. PVC pipe will retain odors, and the dog may get accustomed to his own scent placed on the pipe when he is mouthing it, so you will need to remove the material from the pipe and clean it. You can clean PVC by soaking it overnight in a bleach/water solution (two tablespoons of bleach to one quart of water) and rinsing it thoroughly. This will remove the scent and the pipe will be ready to be used again.

Retrievers love to fetch, but any dog will have fun with this game as part of his training.

You may play fetch using sections of animal hide, but do not use the play skin when you are performing a formal training session. The skin that the dog plays with will have his saliva on it, and he may begin tracking his own scent rather than the scent of the animal. You may take it with you and give it to your dog as a reward, but do not use it in the performance of your tracking sessions.

If you want to teach the dog to give a specific alert such as sitting, scratching, or barking when he finds the scent, you will have to hide the scent tube from him. When he is fetching successfully, start hiding the scent tube so that he can see it but cannot get to it. This can be accomplished by placing it under a plastic bread rack or milk crate. Place the tube under it so the dog can see it, but place something on top of the the crate so that he cannot move it.

If you want your dog to sit as the alert, issue the sit command whenever he locates the source of the scent. Have him hold that position for about ten seconds. At the end of the ten seconds, allow him to get the tube. As you progress in your training, increase the amount of time that he must sit before he is rewarded with the object.

If you want your dog to bark to signal a find, encourage him by not letting him get to the tube. When he emits the first bark, or even a semblance of a bark, allow him access to the tube.

If you want him to scratch when finding the scent article,

which is usually the first thing a dog will do, then do not allow him access to the tube until he scratches at the crate. If you have to show him what you want, do it. Scratch at the crate! Remember, you are going to look foolish when you start, but your dog is going to look like a genius when you are finished.

As always, praise the dog for doing the job correctly. You are paid for the work that you do; the only paycheck the dog gets is your praise. Although this is a less formal form of training, it is still helpful to record your progress in your training log.

Fetch

Your explanation of fetch might sound something like, "When you throw something away from the dog, and he goes to get it and brings it back to you. That's what fetch is!"

In reality, this single command calls for a rather more complicated series of actions. As simple as it is to describe fetch, it involves the dog's understanding of various actions that allows him to accomplish the task. First, the dog has to know how to hold the object that you are throwing. Second, he has to know how to locate it, pick it up, carry it, and give it to you. He has to use his nose and instincts to locate the thrown object so he can bring it back to you. He knows how to use his nose, and the instincts are there, but not all dogs understand the concept of retrieving. You are going to have to help him understand and teach him what it is that you want him to do. Not even all working dogs will retrieve, but if you can direct some of their energy into this game, it makes training the dogs much easier. If you are lucky enough to have a dog that will retrieve on his own, half the work is completed, but you still have to get him to give it back once he has it. Keep in mind that he is not going to learn all of these functions in

Any object used for fetching will acquire the scent of the dog's saliva and will need to be cleaned regularly.

Use an object that interests the dog, one that he will be motivated to keep fetching.

your middle finger and thumb, locate the hinge of the jaw. Press your finger and thumb gently into that joint, which will force the dog's mouth to open. As it opens, place the ball in the dog's mouth, saying, "Take it." He may turn his head away a few times because he is unsure of what it is you are doing, but be persistent, not harsh or brutal. Once he understands that this is not a punishment and that it will not harm him, he will take it in his mouth. Be sure to praise him for taking it by saying "Good boy, good take." This will assure him that he is doing something good and he will be encouraged to comply again.

The next step is to teach your dog to hold the object. Once he has the object in his mouth, lift his head upward so it cannot fall out of his mouth. While doing this, talk soothingly to the dog and tell him to "Hold it." Do not get rough or anxious if he drops it the first few times. Most dogs will not put anything in their mouths and then hold their heads up and back, because they are

one afternoon, so be patient, go at his pace, and the rest will fall into place.

Start with something that will fit comfortably in the dog's mouth, such as a tennis ball or a sponge ball of similar size, or an object such as a light dumbbell that the dog can carry easily. You do not want to start out with anything too heavy, as this will discourage the dog. Hold the ball in one hand in front of the dog, and place your other hand under the dog's lower jaw so that the jaw rests in the palm of your hand. Using unsure of what is happening. When he is more confident that this will not harm him, he will hold the ball. Remember to praise and repeat the command "Hold it."

OK! We have the dog taking the object and holding it. Now you want him to give it back to you. Once he learns how to take and hold it, he may not want to give it back. The same movement you used to open his jaw to place the ball in his mouth may be used to remove the ball. Simply place your hand under his chin, place your thumb and middle finger in the jaw hinge, and press inward. As you do this, tell him to "Give," and take the ball from his mouth when it opens. Do not forget to praise the dog.

Most dogs, once taught this part of the game, will not want to give the object back to you.

An ideal object to fetch is one that fits comfortably in the dog's mouth.

If the object falls on the ground, he may try to get it before you do. If he attempts to pick it up before you do, simply hold his collar and say "Leave it" as you hold him off and pick up the object. If he turns his head so that you cannot get it from him, you will have to be more persistent than he is and retrieve the object from him. He will get the idea, just be patient.

Now that he understands how to take the object, hold onto it, and give it back, he needs to learn how to locate the ball when it is thrown. If he wants to take the ball from you, then you have part of this next section completed. Place a six-foot lead or a long line on the dog's collar. This is your controlling factor, so do not let him take all of it at one time. Hold him at your side and roll the ball about six feet away so that he can see the ball rolling. If he wants to go after it, allow him to do so, but hang on to that lead and give the command "Fetch." As soon as he has the object in his mouth, give the command "Come," and reel him in like a fish. When you get

him back to you, have him sit, and tell him to give the ball to you using your give command.

If he is reluctant to go after the object, take him by the lead and walk him directly to it using the same path, just as you would in beginning the scent training. This helps him identify the path of the ball and the source of the scent. When you reach the ball, give the command "Take it." If he is reluctant to take it, help him by using the methods explained earlier. Once he has it in his mouth, walk him back to the location where you were when you threw the object. Continue this until he wants to go get it and bring it to you.

Now the long line can be extended to its full length. Throw the object and allow the dog to go after it. When he picks it up, call him to you. If he does not come directly to you, then reel him in using the long line. When he gets proficient at this, you can remove the line, and he will begin playing the game.

Each of the above actions should be taught as a separate

function. Take each step individually and spend about three days on each before moving on to the next step. If you try to teach too much in one lesson, he may just give up and fight the lessons. Training each of these steps should only last about fifteen minutes each day. As he begins to grasp one portion of the exercise, move on to another so that you may combine them into one sequence. Once combined, you can play the game of fetch. Each game should last between fifteen and twenty minutes. Playing fetch will help him release some of his pent-up energy and assist in keeping him focused on retrieving. Patience, timing, and consistency are the keys to good training.

You can't keep a good nose off the ground!

You want your dog to be focused on you and ready to learn.

Tracking Lessons

Before going into the field to train your
dog, you must decide which command you will use to get
your dog started. Use of various words or phrases will
help the dog understand what it is that you want him to
do. For example, when you release him at the start of the
track, you may say "Go find" or "Seek." This command
tells the dog that it is time to get started looking for the
source of the track. The choice of words is up to you. It
does not make any difference what the word or command is, as long as you apply that word with its
associative action consistently. Choose words you like
and are comfortable using. Try to select command words
that are uncommon in daily conversations.

A glossary of common commands that you may find
useful in training your dog to perform particular actions
appears on pages 113–115 of this book. This list could
be defined as your dog's own vocabulary and dictionary.
Each word has a meaning and requires a specific action.
Teaching your dog to respond to his own word will make
it easier to train him. If he knows what action is required

by each word, it will ease some of his confusion and your frustration. It doesn't matter if it makes sense to anyone else, as long as your dog knows what is required when he hears it.

Equipment

As you prepare for your first training session, gather all your equipment together. It may seem like a lot to drag around for the first few training sessions, but after a few lessons you will realize it is better to have it when you need it than to interrupt training to retrieve it. You will utilize each of the following pieces of equipment at some point while training or working your dog.

1. Flat collar, to be worn when not working.
2. Two leads, one six feet and one thirty feet. (Half-inch-wide leads are easier to handle.)
3. Long line (fifty feet): A pull cord, the type used on lawn mowers, leaf blowers, and chainsaws (approximately one-eighth-inch diameter), is available at most hardware stores. Attach a bull snap to one end and form a loop handle at the other end. This line is so light that the dog will not know it is on him, and it is strong enough to check his pulling power.
4. Tracking harness, for use when training and working. Be sure to use a tracking harness and not a pulling harness, as you cannot get the proper control of your dog using a pulling harness.
5. Small bell (optional): Placed on a flat collar instead of the tracking harness, the bell should be used when the dog is working. The bell will alert you to where your dog is while he is working off lead, but it will not distract him from his job.
6. Gauze or makeup pads, used to absorb scent from a source.
7. Sealable plastic bags, to store and carry scent material.
8. Three-ring binder, used to maintain training/working log of important information on each dog being trained.

For game tracking, add:
1. Ten to twelve feet of string, for tying to the hide to be pulled behind you.

A choke collar, shown here, is not appropriate for tracking training. A leather lead is recommended only if you can maintain it properly.

2. Animal hide: Rolled squares for laying scent trail.
3. Syringe: A 3 ml/cc syringe containing blood will be used to spread blood scent.

Before you begin training, ensure a proper fit of the harness or bell collar, and practice putting it on and taking it off your dog. This procedure, putting the tracking equipment on your dog, is commonly referred to as dressing the dog. Dressing and undressing will help him become familiar with the equipment and the procedure, and you will not have to struggle with him to get it on when it is time to work.

Consider the type of lead that you'll use. The most appropriate lead is the one that you are most comfortable using, although there are some general differences.

Leather is costly and requires care, such as cleaning and oiling to keep it from drying out. It is going to get wet and dirty in the field, and this is not good for leather. If allowed to dry out, it will crack and eventually break. A leather lead will have to be kept oiled to prevent it from cracking, which can get messy when in use. That said, a leather lead that is properly maintained can last for years.

A cotton lead will be softest on your hands and prevents burning and chafing, but it will dry out, become brittle, and break if it is not properly maintained. When cotton becomes wet, it must be dried and aired. If wet equipment is allowed to dry while folded, the fibers will break down in the folds, rot, and cause the fabric to break. The good thing about cotton is it may be placed in a washing machine for cleaning and may be dried by air or machine. Cotton leads have a tendency to pick up debris as they are dragged, which could mean getting splinters or thorns stuck in your hands.

A nylon lead is the easiest to maintain, but it will cause some burned hands if the dog has a tendency to pull. Nylon leads will require some cleaning and drying, but they withstand rotting better than other materials. It is better to allow nylon to air dry rather than placing it in a dryer. Nylon is not as expensive as leather, and it will last just as long.

The Training Log

The training log is valuable for documenting your dog's training, work, exercise, and health. Completing a log immediately after a lesson (before leaving the work area) will help you remember important things that have taken place during that session. By maintaining your log you will have a reference of your dog's training, his performance, any problems encountered or corrected, and indicators of any need for additional training. Knowing where problems lie allows you to adjust your training to eliminate those problems. In addition to noting the problems, in subsequent logs you should indicate the method of training or adjustments made to correct these problems. Fill out a log every time you work or train with your dog, and place it in a three-ring binder.

Your training log can also become a valuable legal document when signed by a witness. It gives credence to your training schedule and the activities engaged in by you and your dog. If you should ever have to appear in court, you would have a record of the training your dog received, the methods used, problems encountered and corrected, the dog's demonstrated abilities, and the signatures of those who observed the training. Be advised that you should never give up your original records. If requested to bring your records into a courtroom, bring copies of these documents, as the court could hold your records until the completion of an investigation or trial. No one knows how long that may last, and your records could get lost.

Now that you know the importance of the training log, let's discuss the proper way of filling out a log page (see sample on page 65).

The first box on the form is for the dog's name. It is best to place the dog's full name in this box. In other words, if the dog's name is Abney's Sparks a' Flying, do not just write Sparky. Since the log could be deemed a legal document in a court of law, you will want the dog's full name on the document.

The date box is where you will write the day of the week and the date. Again, if called to testify in court, you will want to answer questions as accurately and precisely as possible.

Place the time of day you began your session and the time that it ended. If you have multiple training sessions on a particular day, place the start and end times in the body of the log and in the Time box write "In Log." When writing the times, always place an "S" (for Start Time) in front of your starting time and an "E" (End Time) in front of your ending time, followed by the information about the session.
Example: S -1:30pm – E - 2:00pm.

In the Type box, note the training taking place during this session (such as obedience training, tracking, disaster, conditioning). Noting this helps indicate the intentions of that training session. When you do two types of training, such as tracking and obedience, on the same day, note it in the body of the log, and write "In Log" in the box.
Example: S - 1:30pm – E - 2:00pm – Tracking
S - 2:30pm – E - 3:00pm - Obedience

In the Weather box, note the weather conditions in which you were training or working (such as sunny, raining, cloudy, windy). There are instances when the weather will change during your training session, and noting the changes in the body of the log during training sessions is important.
Example: S - 1:30pm – E - 2:00pm – Tracking – Wind E-3mph
1:45pm, wind shifted to N-8mph and skies became cloudy.

No one is going to expect you to document the exact wind speed, but you should learn the simple 0–12 number system of the Beaufort Wind Force Scale so that you can record a good estimate in this section. A Beaufort chart is provided on pages 110–111.

Indicate the temperature in the box provided, and if there are any sudden changes in temperature during the training session, note them in the body of the log.

Since you will not be training in the same location every time,

write down the general location of the training session. You do not have to give each location from a compass reading, but noting the general vicinity may be useful information.
Example: Pearl River Marsh

Describe the terrain in which you are training or working. Example: Hilly, Flat, Mountainous, Marsh, Swamp, and so on.

Print your name in the Handler box. If you are working with a trainer, or if someone came along to watch your training session, print his or her name in the space provided.

Print the name of the tracklayer or observer in the designated box.

In the Description section, write exactly what you did with your dog from the start of your session to the end of your session. Note all positive and negative training occurrences, as well as the reaction of your dog when encountering an unexpected event. In subsequent training sessions, note what procedure you followed to eliminate or correct the undesirable reaction.

Using this training log will help identify your dog's strengths and weaknesses and what additional training is required. For example, you may have a dog that works excellently in damp, wet conditions and does not mind being on the job. Then again, you may have a dog that does not want to be in such locations. This indicates that you need to provide more work in areas that offer those conditions so he adapts to them. You also have to work under those conditions; if you do not want to do so, or if you display a poor attitude, your dog will read your body language and attitude and respond in kind.

Sign each log as it is completed and have the trainer, observer, and/or tracklayer sign on their respective lines. The signatures make this a legal document, indicating the proficiency of both dog and handler.

I cannot overstate the importance of this document. It is the record of your training, the progress you make, an indicator of problems and solutions, and a history of the work ethic of both you and your dog. Maintaining an accurate training log is crucial to the success of both you and your dog in the world of tracking.

Straightaway Tracks, the First Two Days

Thus prepared, you're ready to begin formal training. When approaching the general search area, your dog should be wearing his everyday collar and a six-foot lead. Maintain control of him so that he does not become a distraction to others in the area. He should not be dressed until he is ready to begin working. Dressing him indicates that it is time to go to work and get serious about the job at hand. Work means fun to the dog, and you will be amazed at how fast he catches on to this.

Take your time dressing the dog, and do not let your anticipation or anxiety affect him. He is an expert at reading your emotions, and he will know when you are excited or anxious. Being too excited may cause him to be more concerned about you than the job he is supposed to be doing.

Every dog has his own method of working and alerting.

Your job is to become familiar with the dog's body language so that you are certain of what he is doing and what he is trying to tell you. Knowing that your dog is actively searching for the trail that you desire will make your training go much easier. Pay attention to his posturing and mannerisms. A stiffened tail, raised ears, and a more determined direction of travel are some indications that your dog is performing his assigned task.

Occasionally dogs are distracted by other scents in the area and may want to investigate those scents instead of working the assigned one. He may begin working on a specific trail but then go looking for something he considers more interesting. We call this behavior "window shopping." You must be aware of the circumstances surrounding the distraction and make the proper correction to ensure that he understands his job. Knowing your dog's body language will assure you that he is on his prescribed course and performing.

One important note should be retained forever—the dog is never wrong. He may become

Training Log

DOG:	DATE:		TIME:
TYPE:	WEATHER:		TEMP:

LOCATION:		TERRAIN:	

HANDLER	TRAINER/ OBSERVER	TRACKLAYER/ OBSERVER

DESCRIPTION:

Handler Trainer/Observer Tracklayer/Observer

distracted by something that raises his curiosity and is more interesting to him. If this happens, you must make a mild correction and put him back on the proper course. Remember, he is using his nose, and if a different, more interesting scent gains his attention, he is still using his nose, so he has not made a mistake. It is your job to make him understand that he must focus on the scent you gave him and ignore all other scents while he is working.

Most mistakes that occur during training are due to handler error. The great majority of those errors come from misreading the dog's body language; reading the dog's body language is something that each handler has to learn, and you will learn by doing as you work with your dog. You need to make adjustments to ensure that these errors do not recur. Make notes in your records by indicating the errors and the actions taken to correct them.

Some of what takes place during training might make you feel silly. I maintain that if you do not feel as if you are making a

fool of yourself, then you are not doing it right. Do not let any feelings of looking ridiculous stop you from training your dog. One thing you must remember is that the lead is like a communication line. Whatever your mood, it will be received by the dog at the other end of the lead. It is important to remain upbeat and happy while training your dog.

For the first few lessons, you will need an assistant who will be required to handle the dog at first before becoming your tracklayer as you and your dog make progress. After the dog understands what you want of him, it is a good idea to substitute other helpers and tracklayers. This assures you that the dog is not looking only for someone he is familiar with, and he understands that he must follow any scent indicated to him.

Whenever I work with a new dog, I always switch the tracklayer. At times I have run short of assistants and have had to ask friends who came to visit to go off into the woods and be my tracklayers. It got to the point at which my friends would say, "If you don't want to see us, just say so. You don't have to send us to the woods." Be sure to explain what you are doing to save those friends who are helping you.

Work into the wind as much as possible when training. The wind will become an aid in driving the scent toward your dog and help him locate the source easily.

Begin by having your assistant handle your dog while you act as tracklayer (see diagram on page 98). You will dress him and attach the long line or tracking lead to him, but the assistant will be the handler. Have the assistant hold the dog by his collar so that he cannot get away while you stand in front of the dog and pump him up. Pumping up your dog is achieved by standing in front of him, bending down and playing with him while saying his name and asking if he wants to go to work ("Buddy, ready to go to work?"). This will encourage him to be excited about doing the work and be eager to come after you when you leave. After pumping up your dog, shuffle your feet so that you make a mark in the earth (scent pad), or drop an article containing your scent (such as a hat, cloth, or shirt) in front of the dog. The article will help him identify the scent path that he needs to follow. Leaving an article for the dog to identify a specific scent is recommended in the beginning stages.

Next, run away from the dog in a straight line while calling his name and encouraging him to come after you. You should stop running approximately seventy-five feet away, in plain view. Turn toward your dog, get down on your knees, and continue calling him to encourage him to come straight to you. This has to seem like a game to the dog, so make it fun.

The handler will tell the dog to "Check" as he passes his hand over the bridge of the dog's nose and points to the scent article you left behind. It is important not to force the dog's head to the article. Since their sense of smell is so acute, forcing his head to the article would be similar to placing a vial of ammonia under your nose. It requires only one sniff for the dog to acquire and retain the scent. Do not spend a lot of time trying to get him to smell it in the same manner that you would. If he appears to have the scent or is struggling to get to you, then just let him work.

The handler will give the command that you have chosen for the dog to start tracking, then release the collar while holding onto the lead. Be sure the handler knows not to push the dog in your direction, but simply to release his hold on the collar as he gives the command. The handler will be required to run behind the dog and feed out the lead gradually so that it does not quickly tighten, which creates the effect of a correction.

The dog should run directly to you. When he arrives, both the tracklayer and the handler should give him both verbal and physical praise. You want him to know that what he did was a good thing. Following the command's completion, and after any exercise, remove the harness as soon as possible. If the dog is allowed to run around or play while wearing his equipment, he will not associate wearing the equipment with work.

If the dog doesn't run directly to you, have the handler stay back from him and guide him to you, using the long line as if flying a kite. Do not force him to come to you, but guide him so that he gets the idea that he has to come directly to you. Forcing him will only make him resent the job, and he will try to avoid you instead of coming to you. Even if he is guided to you, he should receive praise, both physical and verbal, from you and the handler every time he arrives. Repeat these exercises on the first two training days.

Straightaway Tracks, Days Three Through Five

On the third day of training, continue doing all the previous steps, but stop calling the dog. Just go to a spot seventy-five feet away and stand there. The handler will do exactly what he has been doing, which is to give the dog the command to start tracking and to release the dog. If the dog fails to go to you after he is given the command, then you must call the dog to encourage him to track directly to you. Do not advance in training until the dog will come to you after being given his start command and without being called.

Some dogs just want to run all over the place and not concentrate on tracking to you. If this occurs, you will need to slow him down without interfering with his work. With the tracking harness and collar in place, turn the collar so that the "D" ring is under his neck. Pass the line or lead between the harness and the dog's stomach, and attach it to the collar's "D" ring. Now, when the dog is released, hold a steady pressure on the lead while allowing it to extend gradually. This will keep the dog's head close to the ground, help him understand what you want, and slow him down at the same time. Keep tension on the lead, but do not pull so hard that you create the effect of making a correction or cause the dog to flip over.

In straightaway track training, practice a minimum of three repetitive sessions, once a day for five days. You may practice twice each day, but pad these with a four-hour separation between practice sessions. You want to make this a game and not become drudgery for you or your dog.

Diane Lewis © AKC.

Working a straightaway track on the long line.

Tracking dogs learn that they find a reward at the end of the trail, wherever the trail may lead.

In this beginning phase of training, it is okay to work with your dog in the same location, but as you advance in your training it is important to take your dog to various locations. If you conduct all of his training in one location, he will acclimate to that location and will not want to perform elsewhere. By changing the surroundings, the dog will learn that he must work under varying circumstances and despite distractions.

L Tracks, Part One
When your dog is consistently successful at straightaways, you can move on to his second lesson, the L track (see diagram on page 98). At this point, he should understand that the scent you have pointed out to him is what you want him to locate. Since he understands that going directly to you will result in praise or reward, he will work harder to locate the source of the scent.

Prepare for this exercise just as you did for the straightaway. Leave the dog and travel about 100 to 150 feet away, but then make one 90-degree turn to the left or right. Once you have made the turn, find a place to hide out of sight of the dog. Give a signal to the handler to start the dog tracking.

Once the dog is given the command to start, the handler should stop talking to him. Most handlers believe that talking to their dogs while they are work-ing is a means of encouraging them, but constantly talking to a dog will only serve to distract and confuse him. The handler's voice is the source of commands, and if he is constantly talking, the dog will be listening for a command instead of doing his job. Give him a command, and allow him to go to work. If he has a problem that he cannot solve, encourage and help him, but do not continue giving the same command. You should have to talk to your dog only to get him started, to get him back to work if he becomes distracted or after a rest period, and to praise him. It is OK to give him instructions; just avoid constantly repeating them.

The handler should watch the dog closely as he approaches the place where you made the turn. The dog, in his excitement to find you, may overrun the turn. Do not be concerned, as most dogs will do the same thing. If he overruns the turn, allow him time to realize that the scent trail has disappeared and that he will have to use his nose to relocate it. If it appears that he is just looking around and moving away from the scent, check the direction of the wind to ensure that the scent is not being blown in that direction. Give the dog time to figure out what has happened, but do not let him move so far out of the area that he loses interest in locating his prey. In his efforts to relocate the track, he

may see where you are hiding and head straight for you. Do not discourage this action, and remember to praise him once he finds you.

Contrary to popular belief, a dog does not remember where you turned, even if he sees you make the turn. When you disappear from sight, he believes that you have just evaporated. What dogs see is you walking in the distance, and then you just disappear. For this reason, they have to rely on their noses to locate the source. What has happened in this instance is that the dog followed the track until he encountered a turn and began looking for you. Instead of using his nose, he used his eyes. Using his eyes is not a bad thing, but you do want him to use his nose first. As your tracks become longer and turns are more frequent, he will have to rely on his nose to find the source. On the next track, have the handler slow the dog down by holding him back slightly so that he will encounter the turn with his nose. This will help him understand that he will find the source by following the track.

Once the dog realizes that the source has made a turn, he will instinctively look up and scan the area to try to get a visual on the source. If the source is hidden, you will be amazed at how much a dog uses his nose, even to the point of walking right up to the source. Ensure that once the dog makes the turn, he continues using his nose, not his eyes, to locate the source. Do not allow him to run around and look in the hope of seeing the source. Take the precaution of hiding the source well enough that the dog has to use his nose.

To avoid any mistakes during this exercise, the path should be marked so that you are sure that the dog is following it correctly. The tracklayer should mark his turns by placing two sheets of toilet paper over a branch or on the ground to indicate exactly where the turn was made. The handler will know he is on the proper path and will be free to watch the dog's posturing instead of concentrating on the location of the turn.

During an exercise, should your dog lose the track or appear confused, do not get

Air Tracking

Some dogs prefer to follow the scent through air currents rather than ground sniffing. These dogs are referred to as air-scenting dogs. If your dog air scents, be prepared to leave the trail and start plunging through the woods. These dogs do not care about tracks, only the source, and they will take you directly to it once they identify the scent through air currents. If you are doing search-and-rescue work or animal tracking, this is a plus, as air tracking saves a lot of lost time. If you are in competition, however, your dog will have to slow down to stay on the track. To make your dog slow down, pass your long line between the harness and the stomach of your dog and attach the line to the neck collar. Hold tension on the line, and apply a small amount of pressure to bring the dog's head down as he tracks. This will help teach him to keep his nose on the track.

anxious and take him back to the beginning of the track. Instead, take him back to the location where you know for certain that he was tracking. If necessary, take him back to the location of the last toilet paper marker and work from there. Going all the way back to the beginning of the track will only make the dog repeat the same pattern, and he will get bored with the game. This occurs most often in the early stages of tracking because the dog got distracted or found something more interesting. You have to work with him and show your approval each time he does well so that he will forget all of the other things out there. He will do only what you want, just so he can get that special love, praise, and maybe a treat.

This exercise should take about one week for your dog to understand that the scent source will not always go in a straight line. The L track is a very simple exercise and one that can be used to keep the dog in working condition, alert, and wanting to perform. Once the dog is finding you without any distractions or

The long line allows the dog to work far out from you and allows you some control over the dog without pulling him.

wandering about, you may move on to part two.

L Tracks, Part Two

Part two of this lesson is a combination of all previous lessons, except the owner and tracklayer exchange places. The owner of the dog now becomes the handler. Once you reach this point, there is no need for anyone else but you to handle your dog. If you intend for more than one person to handle the dog, this is the time to introduce them to handling. They must use the same commands, gestures, and posture you use, as any inconsistency of wording and body language might confuse the dog.

Working deliberately with his head to the ground is what you want from your dog.

Once you have traded places, begin training with the same sequence of exercises you followed in previous lessons. Start with straightaway searches of about seventy-five feet, and then go on to L tracks. You may discover that when the dog is released he will go directly to the tracklayer without any hesitation. If this happens, move ahead and work on the L tracks. Practice each tracking method for five days. When your dog is following the track and going directly to the tracklayer using both types of tracks without any delays or distractions, you may proceed to the next lesson.

Extended L Tracks and Blood Trails

At this point, some explanation is called for on the differences between tracking humans, locating articles, and competition tracking versus tracking animals or blood trailing. You may go directly to the section of this chapter that pertains to the type of tracking you intend to use; however, you may find information that may be of use to you in your training in each of the sections. I strongly suggest reading the entire chapter.

Human or Article Tracking

When the dog is consistently going directly to the tracklayer without hesitation, you may move on to increasing the distance of the L tracks. Presently you are providing a tracking distance of approximately 100 feet. The tracklayer should extend the distance traveled prior to making the turn and the distance traveled after the turn before finding a hiding place. Keep in mind that you are still doing a basic L pattern but increasing the overall distance traveled to approximately 200 feet.

Do not extend the tracking distances by great leaps, as this could cause the dog to become bored or confused. Dogs have a built-in clock that tells them that they should find the scent source within certain time limits. The dog learns first to find his source in seconds and expects to continue to do so. It is best to extend the distance to the source slowly so the dog will learn gradually that more time is needed to find the source. You will have to help him adjust his built-in parameters by resting or assisting him when he shows signs of fatigue, boredom, or giving up. After he has rested, begin again by giving him a sniff of a scent article and start tracking from the spot where he stopped working.

Competition Tracking

In competition tracking, articles are placed along the track for you to locate and identify. In this type of competition, you do not want your dog to do any air scenting, as he will look only for the strongest source of scent and may abandon the track to locate it. You will want him to keep his head down and stay on the exact track in order for you to locate and identify the dropped articles.

Whenever I do this type of tracking, I substitute a different command to start the dog working. For example, when I want the dog to perform a search, and the track is less important than finding the source, I instruct him with the command, "Go find." When I want him to locate articles and stay directly on the track, I instruct him with the command "Seek." Tailoring the command to the action indicates in this case that I want the dog to stay on the track, locate, and alert me to any article that was dropped along the track.

This type of tracking is much slower, and the dog must be taught to reduce the speed of his search. To slow him down, follow the same procedure described previously for the dog that runs past the tracklayer. If you are using a harness, you should also place the neck collar on your dog. Run the long line along the underside of the harness between the dog's stomach and the harness, and attach the snap to the dog's neck collar. Arrange the neck collar so that the "D" ring is pointing downward. Start your dog tracking with the usual command, such as, "Go find," and then give the command you choose for competition, such as "Seek," immediately after he begins tracking. As you give the command "Seek," put slight pressure on the long line so that the dog's head is pulled downward as he is tracking. If you are not using a harness, then you should place a pinch or prong collar on your dog with the ring pointing downward. Attach your long line to the ring, and run it between the dog's front and rear leg or directly between both front and rear legs and out the back-center of your dog. Again, apply pressure to the tracking lead as you work. This method will teach your dog that he must keep his nose on the trail as he is working and not run off looking for the source. This will also slow him down considerably, so practice until you are certain that your commands produce exactly the response you want.

As you approach an article, allow the dog to reach it first. He must give you an indication (alert) that he has found some-

thing. If you teach him to sit as he finds the article, he will begin sitting and waiting for you to give him the next command after you pick up the article and praise him. You may also teach a bark alert, or almost any other action, for the dog to indicate that he has found something. Once an article is located and praise is given, command the dog to continue by reissuing the seek command, and proceed until all articles are located, an alert is given at each article, and the scent source is found.

At this point, if you are doing human or article tracking, you may skip ahead to the "Show Me" section in the next chapter. If you are doing competition tracking, the "Show me" is optional. In most competitions, your dog will always be on his long line, and you will be there at the same time the source is located.

Animal Tracking
If tracking animals, instead of making a foot pad or leaving a scent article behind, the track-layer will introduce the dog to one of the rolls of the animal skin/hide with a string tied

A Proven Method

Owners who want to teach their dogs to do blood trails for wounded animals may consider this lesson unimportant, but I believe it to be an important first step in helping your dog identify a specific scent and track to it. For those who doubt this method, I include this excerpt from a letter by a former client, Wayne Carlton:

> The first day of tracking class, I harbored a few doubts as to how in the world having my dog sniff the ground and run a few yards to me in a wide open field was going to help it learn to trail a specific deer in the woods. Given the difficulty I sometimes have with the "come" command, I was thankful they ran to me as opposed to taking off (obedience training does work). Keeping in mind that you are good with dogs and train for search and rescue, I had faith and persisted. The dogs became quite good at tracking me, my son, and Rick, but I was still not convinced that this was going to translate into finding a wounded or dead deer. These concerns were allayed the first time you laid out a scent trail using a small piece of deer hide and dribbled blood over it. The dogs' excitement when they came across the blood was impressive. I knew then that they would be able to find a deer.

If you or the dog has difficulty with this lesson, then repeat the straightaway lesson until he is coming to you without any hesitation or deviation. Do not attempt any shortcuts in the lesson, as it will only create confusion for the dog and frustration for you in future lessons. Perform the lessons consistently and you will achieve the required results. Do not doubt the system. It works!

around it. Hold on tightly to the dog's collar and allow the tracklayer to present the skin to the dog so that he may sniff it to get the scent. The tracklayer should play with the dog while using the hide to tease him. The dog may attempt to lick, mouth, or bite at the hide. If he manages to grab the hide, do not scold him, but take it away from him as gently as possible.

While you hold the dog in position, the tracklayer should place the hide on the ground approximately three feet in front of the dog, and step on it. This will put a strong animal scent in front of the dog, and some of the scent will be transferred to the tracklayer's shoe. The tracklayer should then drag the hide by the string as he walks approximately seventy-five feet away. The tracklayer should turn and face the dog and place the hide directly in front of him. When the tracklayer is in position, the dog is given his start command and allowed to run to the tracklayer.

When the dog reaches the tracklayer, direct the dog's attention to the hide. He may mouth it or pick it up. As soon as he grabs the hide, both the handler and the tracklayer should praise him. Have someone hold on to the hide, as you do not want the dog to swallow it. In the excitement of locating it, the dog may attempt to gulp it down, so be prepared to take preventive action. The roll should be too large to swallow, but if he does manage to swallow the hide before you can retrieve it from him, do not try to pull it out. Cut the string immediately and take him to a veterinarian.

The purpose of this exercise is to help the dog recognize that he is in search of the scent from the hide and not the tracklayer. Practice this exercise for approximately five days. When the dog is successfully tracking directly to the tracklayer and hide without hesitation or distraction, you may continue using the same procedure with the L tracks.

Proofing Your Dog

When your dog successfully and consistently locates the handler and hide using the L tracks, you will want to proof him before moving on in training. Proofing is a means of testing your dog to ensure that he has learned the lesson, understands what to do, and performs as expected. If a dog fails a proofing test, then the lesson should be repeated until he can perform.

Proofing may be accomplished by having the tracklayer provide an L pattern, but when he arrives at the chosen location, he should leave the hide, tie the string to a branch or small tree, and return to you instead of waiting there. Do not start the dog until the tracklayer has returned and is standing beside you. This will indicate to the dog that he has to track the scent that is different from those around him. When he locates the hide, both you and the tracklayer should praise him. Practice this new exercise two or three times in each work session.

When you are certain that the dog is locating the hide without any hesitation or being

Diane Lewis © AKC.

German Shepherd Dogs are talented trackers, known for their police and search-and-rescue work.

distracted from the track, you may introduce blood droplets to the tracking procedure. To do this, you should have some blood from a similar animal in a syringe. Remember, blood by itself does not contain the scent of the animal, but it does gather scent as it rolls off the hide.

At the starting point, hold the hide approximately three feet from the dog, but do not step on the hide. Apply some blood to a section of the hide approximately one inch from the edge so that it rolls off the hide and onto the ground. Use enough blood so that four to six drops are on the ground at the starting point. Have the tracklayer walk about fifty feet away while dragging the hide behind him. At this point, the tracklayer should place additional blood on the hide, sufficient to allow two to three drops to fall on the ground. Follow this procedure every 100 feet until the track is completed and the hide is secured. Again, the tracklayer should return to your side before you start the dog on the track.

Pass your hand over the top of the dog's nose, and point to the blood droplets on the ground as you give the command to "Check it." After he has sniffed the blood and he is ready to begin the track, give the command to start him tracking. Bear in mind that as the dog gets closer to the source and can identify its location on air currents, he will often abandon the track and go directly to the source. As he leaves the track, you must be certain that he is going in the direction of the hide and not switching to a different scent or looking around for something that he considers more interesting. The tracklayer should be your guide as to whether or not your dog is following the track and going in the right direction.

You might find your dog is beginning to run faster than you can keep up with. If you slow him down too much, he will think he is receiving a correction. In this case, drop the lead or remove it from the dog, and begin watching him closely as he tracks. He will get ahead and locate the hide before you, so you must attempt to stay as close to him as possible without interfering with his tracking.

When you have achieved tracking blood trails and the dog can locate the source using the L pattern at a distance of 200 feet or more, you may advance to the next lesson.

Z Tracks

The scent article, scent pad, animal skin, or blood droplets will be the starting point of your track. The dog should not be allowed to see the tracklayer leave; he should be brought to the starting point only when it is time to begin the search.

At this level, I strongly recommended that handler and tracklayer use radio communication. Although the first few exercises utilize tracks that are short enough that you are able to call out to the tracklayer, as the tracks become longer you will not be able to hear each other. Yelling to each other will

Curious pups will follow their noses wherever an interesting scent takes them.

give the dog an audible indication of where the source is located. Using radios will help you to stay in communication with the tracklayer in case your dog is unsuccessful during the training session. The tracklayer can also guide you to his location much more efficiently by radio. Remember, there is nothing more embarrassing than having to call the sheriff's search-and-rescue team to help you find your tracklayer.

The Z track (see diagram on page 98) is utilized to teach your dog that turns in a track are to be expected and will occur to the left, right, or both before ending up at the source. Moreover, the zigzag track pattern is the one most often left by lost persons or animals in real-life situations, and it's the one used in most tracking competitions. If an entire length of the track is broken down into segments, you will see a Z-shaped pattern in each segment.

The tracklayer should begin by leaving a scent article, a scent pad, or a few drops of blood rolled off the hide. The tracklayer should then walk straight for fifty to seventy-five feet, then make a turn of greater than ninety degrees to the left or right. After traveling another fifty to seventy-five feet in that direction, the tracklayer should make another turn, again greater than ninety degrees, in the opposite direction. Continue alternating left- and right-hand turns so that there is a minimum of two left- and two right-hand turns on this track. This will be a small challenge for your dog but one that he should be able to master. With these short tracks, the dog should be worked on two separate tracks in each session. You want the dog to work, but you do not want to wear him out on this track or have him lose interest in the game. Allow him fifteen minutes' rest between tracks.

Should the dog have difficulty working this track, reduce the distance traveled from each turn and the amount of time taken to lay the track, then try again. If he continues to have trouble with this exercise, you should either reduce the length of the track or return to working on the L track. Generally, if this occurs, the dog is losing focus on what is expected of him. If you return to the L track, practice both left and right turns until he is tracking them flawlessly. Then you may return to this lesson and continue your training.

After successfully completing the Z track, begin laying tracks that require about five minutes of set-up time. When success is met with that track, advance to tracks that require ten to fifteen minutes to set. Once the dog is successful on tracks that take over fifteen minutes to set, he should be worked only once in each session. If you wish to train twice each day, leave at least four hours between sessions.

Depending on the dog, it generally takes five to ten days for a dog to consistently complete the fifteen-minute track. Do not rush him in an attempt to progress further or faster in training. When the dog does not understand the exercise or is not performing properly, rushing ahead in training will confuse him even more than he already is. Each step is designed to help you read and understand your dog's body language and to help the dog understand the job he has been assigned. Take your

time. You are not in a race to complete your training. By taking your time, you and the dog begin to work as a team, complementing each other's actions and performance. Remember to keep training so that he will perform with you.

The longer the track, the more time there will be for the track to age prior to starting the dog, which will force him to focus on the scent and his job. Continue increasing the tracking distance until the dog indicates that he is tired of the game, quits tracking, or begins to look for other things of interest along the trail. When this happens, you have reached his timing or distance plateau, an internal clock that tells the dog that the game has ended. Rest the dog for at least three minutes and refresh him with the scent article, or return to the location where you saw the last drop of blood or the last place where you are sure he was working.

Most dogs will tire or stop working after thirty to forty-five minutes or after having traveled a distance of one mile. It is up to you to help him through these plateaus. Once you have broken the time and distance barrier, your dog will track until he locates the scent source. Your job will then include observing the condition of your dog while he is tracking, because most will continue searching for the scent source without stopping for a drink or rest unless you make them stop.

Once the dog is tracking to the goal regardless of time or distance, practice a tracking exercise two to three times each week to keep your dog in working condition. Hunters who allow their dogs to spend off-seasons without any training should utilize the Z track two to three weeks prior to hunting season to get their dogs back to their working form.

"Show Me" and Blind Tracks

Now that you are successfully locating the scent source without any difficulty, and while your dog is still on the long line, you will want to teach him to perform a refind. The command for performing a refind is very useful when working your dog off lead. Working a dog off lead

provides for faster location of the source, and knowing that you have a dog that will return to the source after having found it is invaluable.

During training sessions, begin lagging back as you approach the source so that you are at the full extent of the long line behind your dog. Allow him to make the primary alert to the source, but do not rush in to praise or give him any indication that you saw his alert. Instead, call him to you and reel him in on the long line. When he is at your side, take him by the collar, give the command "Show me," and walk him directly to the source. You do not have to follow the same path he used to get to it initially, but you must walk directly to it. When you arrive at the source the second time, give him praise and his reward.

Begin adding the "Show me" command to all of your exercises and, after about one week, he will understand what you want and will walk directly back to the location of the source. Pay particular attention to the fact that he does not run to the source as fast as he did when he first discovered it. He may trot or walk directly and methodically to the source and wait for you to praise him.

As your tracks extend into longer ones, you will find your dog outrunning you in his desire to get to the source. Rather than impede him with the long line, it may be better to remove it and allow him to go on his own. You will have to attempt to keep up with him and keep him in sight as he works. Most dogs will outrun the handler, and watching him can become harder than expected. The best way to keep contact with him is to pay particular attention to the location where he changes direction or disappears from your sight, and then walk directly to that location. Stop and listen for the sound of rustling leaves and branches as he runs, or for the sound of his bell collar. When you determine his location, begin walking toward the sound. He will in all probability return to you to see why you are not keeping up with him. When he returns, give him a command for him to continue working. Do not

use the same command that you used at the start of the track to get him working. Instead, encourage him by telling him "Get to work" or "Where is it?" Repeating the start command once he is working will only confuse him. He is already working, so just give him some encouragement.

Here is an example of how repeating the start command affects your dog. Let us assume your boss gives you a job to do and you begin doing it. He passes by a few moments later and says to you, "Get to work!" You are already working, but he insists that you get to work. A few moments later, he passes by and repeats what he just instructed you to do. This action will annoy anyone, and it will serve the same purpose for your dog. He will begin to lose sight of the command you gave him to go to work. If you have learned to read his body language, you know he is working and simply needs encouragement. If his body language indicates to you that he has found the source, or if you are unsure that he has found the source, you should give him the command "Show me." This will not create any problems, and he will go back to work in an attempt to bring you to the source.

When you have achieved locating and relocating (Show me) the source on known tracks, you are ready to begin working "blind tracks."

Blind tracks are ones in which the tracklayer will leave an indication of where he started the track, but he does not tell you where he will be or how he got there. Radio communication (walkie-talkie) between you and the tracklayer is recommended.

Should you encounter any problems, you will have a means of informing the tracklayer of your situation, and vice versa.

You must rely on your dog and your ability to read him (his body language) in order to locate the source. Here is where the handler will usually make the mistake of trying to second-guess the dog. It is OK, everyone does it at one time or another, but you will soon learn to accept what the dog tells you as being correct, regardless of what you think. You will be amazed at how proficient he is at locating the scent source. Once your dog

Diane Lewis © AKC.

You will be amazed at your dog's abilities and will learn to trust his nose as the two of you progress in your training.

proves to you that you are mistaken in your second-guessing, you will never do it again.

If your dog should fail to follow a track or locate the source on a blind track, you should take one step backward in training. Return to locating known tracks until you are certain that you can read your dog and have eliminated any problems.

Contamination and Distractions

There will be times when your track will not be as clean or sterile as you would like. People will be walking along your track in order to assist you, while other animals may cross the track, leaving scents behind to intermingle with the one your dog is working. There may be litter, toys, and other distractions left behind by others who were previously in the area. Since there is no way of telling when you may face these distractions, it is best for you to incorporate possible diversions into your practice work.

Allowing the track to age is one way to challenge your dog,

and you will want to also add a contamination factor. One method of contaminating a track is to have numerous people walk over the track left by your track-layer from the starting point up to approximately the first turn. These people's scents will be fresher than the one your dog is tracking, and overcoming these distractions will be invaluable. When he is successfully working in a track that has been contaminated by people, bring their dogs to the track and repeat the contamination scenario by walking their dogs over the top of your assigned track. A section of hide from a different animal can also be dragged along your track to add to contamination. If you encounter any other distractions while performing a search that you think your dog should know to avoid, simply add them to your practice tracks.

After working through contamination at the beginning of your track, you will want to add distractions and contamination throughout the entire track. Begin by having others hold their dogs on lead approximately twenty feet from where you are

Human

The best time to begin a search for a missing or lost person is as soon as humanly possible. The sooner you can get to the scene, the better. All too often, people go out looking for a lost or missing person, or call for assistance from the local law enforcement agency, and they do more harm than good. They contaminate the track that was left behind, and if they find any article or clothing, they have a tendency to pick it up and mishandle it, often rendering it useless as a scent article.

You want the scent article to be as pristine as possible. Using a person's pillowcase or article of clothing that has been worn, but not placed in with other clothing, is the best article you can use.

Time is of the essence when searching for lost people. You never know what they may have encountered. You do not know if they are sick or injured, preventing them from returning home. The weather elements play a major factor in the welfare of the person who is lost. Hyperthermia or hypothermia may be a factor, and that will reduce the amount of time available to rescue the person safely from his or her location.

While searching for people, look for signs of their presence in the area, such as a candy wrapper, cigarette butt, drink can or bottle, clothing, body fluid or excretions, and such. All of these are indicators that you are on the right path.

You must work diligently and expeditiously. If you or your dog is having a problem in locating the track or maintaining a good trail, then ask for assistance. Never let your pride come between you and the rescue of a person. It is important to be a part of the team that rescues, and not to be the person who hampered it.

Know your dog and know your limitations. Never be afraid to say, "I don't know," and pass it off to someone who does. You will learn what you did not know, and that will make you a better rescuer in the future.

With all of that said, you must treat every search as if it were a crime scene. You never know what you will be walking into, and you must be able to walk out of it. If it happens that it does become a crime scene, you must notify the authorities of where you and your dog were physically, and identify everything you touched. Failure to make this notification could place you at the scene as a suspect, instead of as an assistant to the search.

Wounded Animals

The majority of hunters who wound an animal begin searching for that animal immediately after it has been shot. If you are going to use a dog to locate the wounded animal, the best course of action is to wait before tracking.

Make a note of where the animal was when it was shot, identify and mark any place where you may find blood, and leave the area. Go back to the hunting camp and have a cup of coffee. Wait a minimum of thirty minutes before you begin tracking. Why should you wait? The answer to that question is that once an animal has been wounded, it will run on sheer adrenaline. Even though it may be dying, it will continue to run. The reason for waiting is to give the animal time to relax and lie down. There is no rush to find it. If the wound was not a fatal one, then it will be gone, and you will not have wasted a lot of time looking for something that was not there.

When it is time to begin the search, dress your dog at the start of the track. Do not put his bell collar or harness on him at the camp and then walk him through the woods. That action will only serve to confuse him. Wait until you are in the area that you marked prior to dressing him.

Once he is dressed, talk to him. Ask him if he is ready to go to work. You want to make him excited about the job he is about to do, and you want that job to seem like a game. Next, take him to the
(Continued on next page)

location of the blood, and allow him to sniff. If he begins pulling away from you prior to reaching the exact spot, he is indicating that he already has the scent and is ready to begin. If he waits for you to show him what you want, simply bring him to the area and, holding his collar, pass your hand over the top of his nose and point directly to the spot of blood. As he puts his head down to sniff, give him his command to go to work. Remember, it takes only one sniff for him to identify the scent that you want him to locate, so do not keep him at that spot for too long.

I recommend taking your dog on the track of a known downed animal. This will reinforce the command, the work, and the find. The first time a dog finds a completely intact animal, he may bolt or jump back from it. This is normal and there is no need to be concerned about his behavior. He has been tracking on small sections of hide, and now he is finding the real thing.

If you have allowed your dog to work off lead, you will need to be sure that he understands the "Show me" command, and you must be able to read your dog's body language. Once he finds the prey and returns to you, if you do not understand what he is telling you, he may just go off and play. In that case, you will have to call him and have him do the search all over again. This is very boring to a dog, and performing that task repeatedly will only give him cause to quit working.

We all thrive on praise, and for a dog praise must be both verbal and physical. It needs to last only three seconds, but you must put your hands on the dog and praise him, saying, "Good boy" while doing so. If you forget to praise your dog, he may shut down and not want to play this game any more. Your praising the dog is just as important as his finding that scent source.

going to begin. They should engage in conversation with each other or be playing with their dogs. There should be a person positioned along the track approximately one-third from the beginning of the track, and another should be approximately one-third from the end. The person may be walking, standing, or sitting. The purpose of this exercise is to simulate meeting someone different from the scent you are tracking. It is OK for the dog to investigate the person, sniff, or approach him or her. Allow the dog a few seconds to determine that this is not his scent source and move ahead.

Should the dog give an indication on any of the distractions, you must stop tracking, give a fresh scent from a scent article, and bring him back to a point where you know he was tracking properly or to the last place you saw blood droplets. Most dogs will ignore the distractions, but some will tire of the game and want to find something more interesting. You must work him beyond these distractions. Do not chastise the dog, because he has not done anything wrong. He has

Diane Lewis © AKC.

You are being trained along with your dog as the two of you work together and you learn to read his body language.

located a scent source, but not the one you want.

Once your dog has successfully completed a track with distractions, you will teach him scent discrimination. This is accomplished by having three people start at the same location. One will be your tracklayer, and the others will be decoys. As they leave the starting location, have them crisscross each other's tracks by switching places as the tracklayer lays the appropriate track. After making a few turns, have the two decoys turn in opposite directions and return to the starting point without walking over the track on their return. Have the decoys remain out of sight of your dog. When the tracklayer is in position and has given you the assigned signal, begin tracking.

You will want your dog to track directly to the tracklayer and ignore the decoys' tracks. This is where radio communication becomes a valuable tool. The decoys can convey where they turned off the track, or your tracklayer can assist you should your dog make the wrong decision. When your dog has located the tracklayer, take your dog back to the location where the decoys turned, and choose one of them. See if your dog can track one of the decoys back to the starting point.

When you and your dog are locating multiple tracklayers, you will have to rely on information that you gain from the first tracklayer. Ask which direction the other tracklayers went. If the first tracklayer is found and is unable to direct you toward where the others have gone, look around for another set of tracks or a scent article that may have been dropped. If you do not find any clues, place a short lead on your dog and begin walking him in ever-widening circles away from the first tracklayer and the track that brought you to him. When your dog recognizes the scent, give his command to begin tracking. Continue until all tracklayers are found.

You will be amazed to see your dog track between multiple scents when he is made aware of which one you want him to locate. I once observed a dog track up to eight people within a diameter of two miles before tiring and needing to be replaced by another dog. Once your dog understands what you want from him, he will work until you stop him or he runs out of stamina.

If you are tracking blood trails, be sure that the tracklayer is leaving the blood droplets intermittently along the track as you did when you first began blood trails. There will be times when you will have blood only at the beginning of your track or a drop or two along the track, and then it will stop. To prepare for this, the tracklayer should stop leaving droplets at a point approximately one-third of the way to the completed track.

As an aid to your dog, it is advisable to use a gauze pad to absorb some of the blood from your starting point and place it in a sealable bag. If your dog should lose the track or become distracted, you will have the source sample to reinvigorate his senses.

The X Track

The X track (see diagram on page 99) is encountered when a subject travels some distance,

changes direction, and then changes direction again so that he crosses over the first section of the track. If the entire track were drawn on paper, it would resemble the letter X. These X tracks are often erroneously referred to as backtracking. In a backtrack, however, a subject turns and retraces his steps over the original path, then at some point along the track departs in a completely different direction.

X patterns can be confusing to handlers who have not experienced a dog discriminating on a stronger, or hotter, scent along a track. The well-trained dog will recognize the most recently laid scent and track that scent. If the subject has crossed over the original track, the dog will choose the (hotter) scent and continue tracking in the new direction. More often than not, handlers who have seen the subject traveling in one direction will acquire a mind-set that the track must be followed. They will insist that their dog continue tracking the direction known to the handler, but the dog will want to track the newer scent.

This is when handlers make

Coursing

During a search, most dogs put their noses to the ground and run while checking for scent along the track. Sometimes it will appear to you that in this posture they are not watching where they are going and are about to run head-on into a tree. Do not be alarmed. They know what they are doing and where they need to be going, and are aware of the trees.

If your dog air scents all the time, he will be the one to locate the scent source the fastest; however, there will be times when you want him to search a scent path. This is when knowing how to course will come in handy.

Using standard cardboard boxes, begin laying out a course. You may use as many boxes as you desire. Place the boxes approximately thirty to fifty feet apart to give you room to move about and prevent any confusion. Once the dog learns the coursing procedure, you may place the boxes side by side, and he will choose the one that contains the scent.

In order to assist your dog in learning to course, he will have to wear a harness. Weave your twenty-foot lead through the underside of the harness, and connect it to the dog's flat collar. Do not use any type of chain or pinch collar. You are going to be guiding him, but you do not want him to perceive your guides as corrections. As he begins to search, gently put tension on the lead, causing his head to be pulled downward. This will teach him that you want him to check the ground for scent and not just run to the source.

Begin dragging your scent article from the start point to the first box, and continue going from box to box. Place the scent article under the last box. Bring your dog to the start point where you began dragging the scent and, keeping him on lead, release him with your working command. Guide him toward the first box and allow him to investigate the box for approximately fifteen seconds. Proceed to the second box and repeat the process. Proceed from box to box until he reaches the box with the scent article under it. Wait for him to give you an alert, and then praise him both verbally and physically.

Using the pattern below, you may determine whether your dog is air scenting or tracking. Begin at the starting point and release the dog without his lead. If he runs directly to where the source is hidden, then he is air scenting. If he goes from box to box, he is tracking (coursing).

When he becomes proficient at coursing, lay out the course, but place the scent article under different boxes. You may witness him running through the course, then changing direction or turning around to return to the one containing the source. This is OK, and you must praise him for doing his job.

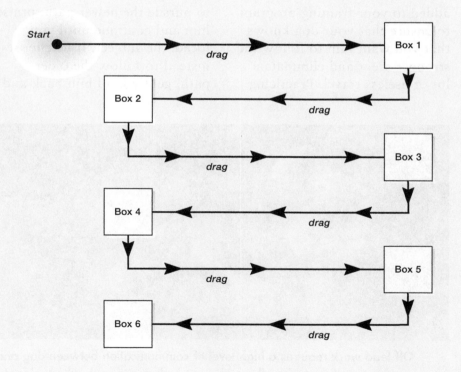

the mistake of trying to correct their dogs. You must place all of your confidence in your dog, and you must be able to read his body language. Even though the track continues for some distance from where the dog has changed direction, you must trust that the dog has made the right decision. His nose will detect the crossing of the tracks, and he will choose the proper one.

The X track should be added to your training program to ensure that your dog knows that you want him to follow the stronger scent and eliminate a lot of useless travel. Practicing on this type of track pays off, as it eliminates following a complete track when the time spent finding the subject could have been shortened by following the dog. Your track-layer should mark the track so that you know where the path has been crossed. When your dog approaches this juncture, allow him the time he needs to assess the scent and choose a direction to follow. If he wants to pursue the newer path, praise him and continue until you locate the subject. If he chooses instead to follow the older path, gently hold him back and

Off-lead work requires a high level of communication between dog and handler; you must understand each other's signals.

assist him in locating the proper track.

The X track is the one most often used in pursuit of wounded animals and escaped prisoners, both of whom deliberately circle an area and cross over their previous tracks in an attempt to confuse or lose their pursuers.

The Circular Track

The circular track (see page 99) is the most confusing of all to both the handler and the dog, but is a common pattern in real-life situations and thus important to master. A wounded animal will circle in an attempt to confuse its adversary. Hunters who get lost often unknowingly travel in a circle in an attempt to find their way out.

Circling presents a problem for the dog because a relatively large amount of scent is distributed in close proximity. Scent is shed along the perimeter of the circle and naturally pools toward the center. Due to the pooling effect from all directions, the scent becomes so strong that the dog believes he is near the source. He will continue trying to locate the source by following the scent and staying within the circle. Circular tracks that are approximately twenty-five yards or less in diameter pose the greatest challenge.

When you realize that you have searched the same location more than once, you are probably within a circular track. The handler must place his lead on the dog and walk in ever widening circles, away from the center, until the barrier is broken. Continue walking him until he gives an indication that he has found the scent outside of the circular location. When you have cleared the barrier, the dog will begin looking for the scent trail again.

As he begins to track, be certain that he is not on the scent leading back to where you began tracking. In trying to make sense of confusing signals, he may attempt to backtrack or return to the circled area. Do not rush to remove his lead until you are certain that he is moving away from the circle. Allowing him to begin searching off lead too soon may free him to return to the area that he knows had the strongest scent, and you will have to begin the process again.

The Straightaway

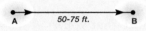

This is the first step to be taken. Have the dog sniff the hide, and then leave to a position, dragging the hide, to a point that is directly in front of him, at approximately 50–75 feet away. Have another person hold the dog until you are in place. Have the person give the command and release the dog. The dog is to be released, and not shoved in any direction. Give the command and release the dog.

The L

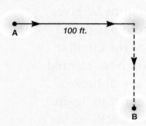

Using the same technique and/or dragging the hide, move away from the dog in a straight line approximately 100 feet, turn either left or right, and go to a place where the dog cannot see you. The dog is given his command, released, and allowed to begin his search. This is an important step. The dog must understand that scent will turn. Do not proceed until this pattern is performed with complete accuracy. If the dog has any trouble working in an L pattern, return to the Straightaway test.

The Z

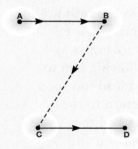

This pattern is the same as that of a wounded animal or escapee attempting to throw off its trackers. Movement is similar to the L but angles away from the turn and back again while moving in the same general direction. When the dog is proficient at this, begin the X.

The X

This is the pattern used when attempts are made to backtrack to a safe haven. You may follow what appears to be a clean track and then cross over a section that was covered previously and continue into another area. Follow the letters by leaving point A and travel to point B. Then cross over to point C, and end up at point D.

NOTE: Do not be surprised if your dog does not follow the entire track. When a dog becomes proficient at tracking, he will note where the scent is freshest. For example, he may leave point A and, upon entering the junction where all lines meet, choose to go in the direction of D. This is OK. Your dog has determined the freshest (hottest) scent and will go in that direction, saving you lots of footsteps.

The Circle

This is the hardest and the most common. Humans and animals will go to an area and circle, either because of confusion or to lose the pursuer. When circling, a pocket of scent is formed in the center of the circle. This is referred to as "pooling." When the scent pools, it is as if the animal were standing in front of the dog. If you find your dog making circles or you see yourself coming back to the same spot, it is time to place the lead on your dog and begin making ever-widening circles to help the dog find the scent that leaves the circle. Make certain that you do not allow the dog to exit the circle from the point where you originally entered the circle; otherwise, you will be heading back to the point where you began your search. Instead, allow the dog to leave only at a junction where the scent is going away from the circle. Once you are certain that you are on the right track, release your dog again, and give the search signal.

You must be prepared to provide proper health care from the moment you bring your pup home and for his entire life.

First Aid for Tracking Dogs

Long before you begin tracking with your dog—in fact, as part of your preparations for bringing a puppy into your home—you should know the location of the nearest emergency veterinary hospital. Too many owners wait until there is an emergency before trying to find such a facility. Since veterinarians do not work twenty-four hours a day, it is important that you know where you can bring your dog if the need arises. Ask your veterinarian what his procedure is in the case of off-duty emergencies.

   If at any point you have to perform first aid on your dog, know that even a beloved pet could bite you if he is in pain. A quick muzzle (cloth muzzle designed for short-term use) is advisable and is well suited for these situations.

Allergic Reactions

Some dogs have allergic reactions to bee stings or other insect bites. If your dog suffers such a reaction, you may administer Benadryl at a rate of $1/2$ mg per pound of body weight. This may slow the reaction and calm the dog.

Working in cover and wooded areas can expose a dog to certain injury-causing risks.

Signs of severe reactions include watery and itching eyes, swollen face, sneezing, difficulty in breathing, and unconsciousness. In case of severe reaction, transport the dog to your veterinarian or emergency facility immediately.

Bleeding

Minor lacerations can be flushed with 0.9 percent sodium chloride and betadine solution or chlorhexidine solution. If these are not available, lacerations may be flushed with clean water and washed with antibacterial soap. Flushing should continue until all visible foreign material, such as dirt and debris, are removed. After flushing the wound, apply an antibiotic ointment and a bandage.

Severe lacerations may involve injury to muscles, tendons, ligaments, and blood vessels. To control bleeding, apply direct pressure to the wound using your hand and gauze pads or a clean cloth. If there is any doubt about whether a laceration needs sutures, cover the wound and bring the dog to the veterinarian for treatment.

Internal bleeding can be caused by an external injury, disease, or infection. Generally there is no sign of bleeding, but symptoms such as fainting, rapid or shallow breath, and weak pulse are indicators of an internal problem. Blood may sometimes be visible in urine or feces or expelled from the nose or mouth. If any of these signs or symptoms is visible to you, bring your dog to your veterinarian immediately.

Bloat

Bloat can occur within minutes, so time is of the essence. Bloat is more commonly seen in larger, deep-chested breeds, but it can occur in any breed. One common cause of bloat is running or exercising directly after eating. The solid, heavy, undigested food causes the stomach to flip over, twisting the intestines closed. Gas cannot escape and builds up in the stomach.

Signs of bloat include burping, an enlarged abdomen, pacing, heavy panting, a growling stomach, attempted vomiting, and heavy salivation. The dog may refuse to lie down because of pain in the prone position. The dog may continually turn to check his rear end and may lick at the anus. Transport the dog to your veterinarian or emergency facility immediately, as surgery is almost always necessary.

Breathing (CPR)

To assist your dog's breathing (resuscitation), pull the tongue out of his mouth and clear the throat of any obstructions. Keep his neck and head as straight in line as possible without causing any further injury. Close his mouth and, making a seal around his nose,

give two full breaths. If the breaths go in easily, continue with the assisted breathing at a rate of ten to fifteen breaths per minute, and transport him to the nearest veterinarian or animal emergency room. If there is difficulty getting the breaths to go in, check the dog's mouth for any foreign objects that may be obstructing his airway. Remove them and begin the breathing again. If there aren't any objects or if attempts to assist with breathing are still not working, make a fist with one hand and place it against the stomach. With both hands, lift the dog so that his rear legs are off the ground. Give three to five sharp, rapid, upward thrusts. Reposition the head and neck and attempt breathing again.

Burns

Because of the high risk of infection, burns should not be treated with any topical solutions. Instead, use cold or tepid water on the burn, cover the area, and transport the dog to your veterinarian or emergency facility.

Car Accident

The very first thing to do if your dog is hit by a moving vehicle is to place a quick muzzle on him. Well-meaning efforts may be misread by the dog, causing him to bite out of fear, disorientation, and pain. Do not attempt to stabilize any fractures. Gather any dismembered parts, place them on ice, and bring them with you. Keep the dog warm with a blanket or jacket, place him on a rigid board, and transport him to your veterinarian or emergency facility immediately. Tie a tourniquet around any areas that are bleeding severely.

Choking

For medium to large dogs, follow the instructions in the section on Breathing (CPR). If the object is not expelled after your thrusts, inspect the dog's mouth to see if the object is visible. Do this by carefully pulling the dog's tongue out of his mouth and looking inside. If an obstruction is visible, remove it with your fingers.

For a small dog, you must sit down and place him astride one knee so that his stomach is against your knee. With your hands on his back, carefully give three to five sharp thrusts downward against your knee. You must use caution so as not to cause any back injuries.

Foot Injuries

The majority of foot injuries occur to the foot pad, which cannot be sutured. Apply pressure to the wound until all bleeding stops. Cleanse the wound with soap and water and dry well. Bandaging the foot is advisable; however, most dogs will chew the bandage off of the foot. Another method of protecting the injury is to apply Super Glue to the outer edges of the injury and hold the wound closed until the glue dries. Caution must be taken to avoid gluing yourself to the dog. Once the glue has dried, the wound will be protected, and the dog may move about freely. As the wound heals, the glue will wear off through normal walking.

Fractures

Fractures can be temporarily stabilized by wrapping a rigid splint to the fractured site or by applying a thick padded bandage. Make sure the splint or bandages extend above and below the fracture. Be careful not to wrap the splint too tightly. Any swelling of the foot on the fractured leg may be an indication that the splint is too tight. Loosen the splint slightly and observe the swelling. If the swelling begins to subside, do not retighten the splint. Open or compound fractures, where the bone may be seen exiting a wound, require immediate medical attention.

Don't ignore the signs if your dog appears to be getting overheated.

Gunshot Wounds

All gunshot wounds should be examined by a veterinarian. Wounds caused by long-range shotgun blasts are generally less severe, as the pellets will lodge beneath the skin without causing internal injury, and thus have less medical urgency. Handgun and rifle injuries produce a stronger force of penetration and may be life threatening. Even if visible entrance and exit wounds show that the bullet has passed through cleanly, unseen tissue damage may be severe. Bones and cartilage may have been broken or splintered, which may cause further harm and infection. Attempt to stop all bleeding, and transport the dog to your veterinarian or emergency facility.

Head Injuries

If your pet sustains a head injury that renders him unconscious, do not attempt to revive him. Place a cold cloth on his head, and transport him to your veterinarian or emergency facility. As the dog revives, disorientation is common.

Check your dog's eyes and ears for foreign matter or signs of injury after time spent working in tall grasses and brush.

Heat Stroke

The most common signs of heat stroke include rapid panting, accelerated heart rate, red and dry mucous membranes, and possible vomiting and diarrhea. Dogs may appear weak and disoriented. The most important first aid that can be administered is to cool the dog. Soak the dog with cool water in a bathtub or pond. Continue to soak the dog until you obtain a rectal temperature reading of 103 degrees Fahrenheit. In the field, cooling the dog may also be accomplished by wetting down the undersides of the legs closest to the body, the neck, and the nasal areas. If the dog will drink, give him pediatric electrolytes. Severe effects of a heat stroke can manifest themselves after the temperature is lowered, so it is recommended that the dog be checked by a veterinarian.

Be attuned to your dog's behavior during hot, humid days, as severe overheating can result in hyperthermia, which can be fatal. A sign of hyperthermia is a widening of the tongue, which hangs far out of the mouth. There also may be saliva dripping from the tongue. Wet footprints caused by perspiration may appear where the dog walks.

Hypothermia

This is dangerously low body temperature, the opposite of

hyperthermia. A dog that suffers from hypothermia may seek shelter from the wind and cold and curl into a ball. Move him to a warmer location, and cover him with blankets to keep him warm. Warm him slowly because if the dog is warmed too rapidly, it will cause him to go into shock. Hypothermia can kill if you don't recognize the symptoms and take steps to remedy the condition.

Poison

Poisoning can be caused by insecticides, lye, cleaning fluids, certain varieties of plants, and automobile antifreeze. Antifreeze is extremely dangerous because dogs are attracted by its sweet taste and because even small quantities can be fatal. If you know what your dog has ingested, you may choose to induce vomiting. This can be accomplished by orally administering syrup of ipecac or about four ounces of hydrogen peroxide. Some poisons such as petroleum products, acids, caustic chemicals, or alkaloids are more dangerous if vomiting is induced. Follow the advice of

Canine First Aid Kit

Quick muzzle
Scissors
Tweezers
Cotton
Small empty container
Rectal thermometer
Gauze pads and bandages
Adhesive tape
Bottled water
Hydrogen peroxide
Rubbing alcohol
K-Y or petroleum jelly
Antibacterial ointment
Activated charcoal
Castile soap
Furicin powder
Kaopectate
Syrup of ipecac

your veterinarian, or contact the Poison Control Hotline for Animals.

If you suspect that your pet may have been exposed to something toxic, either internally or externally, the following phone number will connect you with an ASPCA veterinarian specially trained to assist pet owners or other veterinarians. This is the only dedicated animal poison control hotline in the world manned by veterinarians, not telephone operators. The number is staffed twenty-four hours a day, seven days a week: (888) 4AN-HELP or (888) 426-4435.

Pulse

Dogs have a carotid pulse, but it is difficult to palpate. To obtain a pulse, place your fingers in the inner crease of the femur, located on the hind leg just below the groin and above the stifle, and press lightly against the bone. You should be able to feel a pulse.

Punctures

Any wound that has penetrated the thorax or abdomen should be treated by a veterinarian immediately. If the object causing the wound is still intact, do not remove it from the wound. Simply protect the wound as much as possible by wrapping gauze around the object next to the wound, and bring the dog to the nearest veterinarian or emergency clinic. In the case of a sucking wound, one where you can actually hear air escaping the

wound, cover the wound with a cloth coated with furacine ointment or petroleum jelly and seal off the wound. Get the dog to a veterinarian or emergency clinic immediately.

Shock

A dog may go into shock due to injury, loss of blood, or exposure. Treat shock by keeping the dog warm and comfortable. Never give any medication to a dog that appears to be in shock. Symptoms of shock are cold to the touch, labored breathing, gums appearing white in color, and unconsciousness. Transport the dog to your veterinarian or emergency facility immediately.

Snakebite

Most venomous snakes inject toxins that cause tissue necrosis (tissue death). Local signs include bleeding puncture wounds, severe pain, and swelling at the site, although swelling may be minimal. Tissue in the affected area may then become necrotic and be sloughed off or require debridement (surgical removal). The best course of action is to bring the dog to a veterinarian immediately. Severe systemic effects, infection, and death may occur. In the field, 10 to 25 mg (approximately ½ mg per pound) of Benadryl can be given and may serve to calm the dog. Infection is another common problem with snakebite and may require treatment with systemic antibiotics.

Stress

Stress is often overlooked as the cause of personality or temperament changes. A normally happy-go-lucky dog suddenly turns into an aggressive animal. Temperament changes are one of the signs of stress. Others include, but are not limited to, loss of attention, slow responses to commands, loss of appetite, and diarrhea. Possible causes of stress include overtraining, overworking, unpredictable situations, dog shows, crowds, and unfamiliar surroundings. Anticipate the latter following a family move to a new home. Proper nutrition and socialization will help reduce stress.

Your dog may come face-to-face with any number of critters that make him stop in his tracks.

The Beaufort Wind Force Scale

The Beaufort Wind Force Scale was devised in its earliest form in 1805, when British Commander Francis Beaufort sought to identify the effects of wind force on a man-of-war (fighting ship). By 1838, the scale was mandatory on all Royal Navy ships. In 1912, the International Commission for Weather Technology sought agreement on a standardized scale, which was accepted in 1926 and revised in 1946.

Although adopted for use on ships, the scale was also useful to meteorologists. Knowing and understanding the gradual effects of wind on land and sea will be valuable to you in estimating the wind speed in which you are training and working.

The wind properties listed here correspond to a simple numeric range from 0 to 12 . The scale number signifies the wind's name as identified by meteorologists, wind speed in miles per hour, and visible effects on land and sea. Referring simply to the scale number eliminates the need to write a detailed description in your training log.

Beaufort #	Name	Miles per Hour	On Land	On Sea
0	Calm	< 1	Calm, smoke rises vertically	Sea like a mirror
1	Light Air	1–4	Direction of wind shown by smoke drift, but not by wind vanes	Ripples but without foam crests
2	Light Breeze	5–7	Wind felt on face; leaves rustle; ordinary vane moved by wind	Small wavelets; crests do not break
3	Gentle Breeze	8–12	Leaves and small twigs in constant motion; wind extends light flag	Large wavelets; scattered whitecaps
4	Moderate Breeze	13–18	Raises dust and loose paper; small branches are moved	Small waves; frequent whitecaps
5	Fresh Breeze	19–24	Small trees in leaf begin to sway; crested wavelets form on inland waters	Moderate waves; many whitecaps
6	Strong Breeze	25–31	Large branches in motion; telephone wires whistle; umbrellas used with difficulty	Large waves; white foam crests, probably spray
7	Near Gale	32–38	Whole trees in motion; inconvenience in walking against wind	Sea heaps up; white foam blown in direction of wind
8	Gale	39–46	Breaks twigs off trees; generally impedes progress	Moderately high waves; crests break into spindrifts
9	Strong Gale	47–54	Slight structural damage occurs; chimney pots and slates removed	High waves; dense foam; crests roll over; visible spray
10	Storm	55–63	Trees uprooted; considerable structural damage occurs	Very high waves; surface appears white; heavy tumbling
11	Violent Storm	64–72	Very rarely experienced inland; accompanied by widespread damage	Exceptionally high waves; long white patches of foam; visibility affected
12	Hurricane	73 +	Widespread damage to devastation	Air filled with foam spray; sea completely white with driving spray; visibility seriously affected

Glossary of Commands

About—The dog's return to the heel position after a recall (*see* Finish, Heel).

Aus (German)—Out.

Back (or Back up)—To move in a backward direction from the present position. This is useful when turning in confined areas.

Bad dog—Verbal reprimand given when the dog has deviated from a learned behavior but a physical correction is not in order.

Bleib (German)—Stay.

Bring—Given to have the dog bring an object to you.

Catch—1. Used to have the dog grab an object before it hits the ground. 2. Fetch a moving object (*see* Fetch).

Check—Given when you want the dog to sniff in a specific area that you have pointed to. Useful when working scenting dogs to help them pinpoint the scent they are looking for.

Climb—Used when walking up ladders or stairs.

Come—Used when the dog should stop whatever he is doing and return to the handler. Also referred to as a call or recall (*see* Heya).

Cookie—Offering a food reward for something done right. Generally used in the form of a question. "Do you want a cookie?" (*see* Treat)

Crate—Used to have a dog enter his crate, as in "Get in your crate" (*see* House, Kennel, Yard).

Cut—Used to break up fights. Spoken in a loud, deep, throaty, and harsh fashion. This is a derivative of the expression "Cut it out" and utilizes the "K" sound. Use the word as you move toward the battling pair. I believe that this word, when spoken in a harsh manner, makes the two dogs in conflict believe that the bigger dog (you) is going to enter the battle, and it helps stop the fighting.

Down—Lie down in a prone position (*see* Platz).

Drop it—Release what you are holding (*see* Give).

Easy—Used to slow down the speed (*see* Slow).

Fast—Used to speed up (*see* Hurry up).

Fetch—1. Retrieve an object that has been thrown. 2. Look for an object (*see* Seek, Sook).

Finish—1. Return to the heel position after a recall. 2. Used to indicate the completion of a job (*see* About, Free dog, Heel, OK).

Five—Used when you want a dog to shake hands with you (*see* Paw, Shake, Foot).

Foos (German)—Heel.

Foot—Used to examine the feet (*see* Five, Shake, Paw).

Free dog—Work is completed and he is free to do whatever he pleases (*see* Finish, OK).

Friend—1. Indicating a new acquaintance is friendly. 2. Search for a cadaver (death) scent.

Give—Release what is in your mouth (*see* Drop it).

Go find—1. Look for your toy. 2. Used for locating lost or missing people.

Good—Verbal praise for a correct response.

Go play—You are finished your job and free to play (*see* Free dog, OK).

Go to—Go in a direction or toward a person or object that has been pointed out (*see* Visit).

Heel—By your left side. This is used to have the dog go into motion with you or sit at your side. It may also be used to have the dog return to the heel position after a recall (*see* About, Finish, *Foos*).

Heya (German)— (*pronounced hee-ya*) Come.

Home—Backtrack to the starting location. This is helpful when you have completed your search. The dog knows the track much better and can take you back to camp.

House—Go to your sleeping quarters or doghouse.

Hurry up—1. Used to speed up work (*see* Fast). 2. Perform natural body functions.

In—Enter an enclosed object, structure, or building.

Jump—Get on or get over. Leap to or from.

Kennel—Go to the kennel or sleeping quarters, as in "Kennel Up" or "Kennel" (*see* Crate, House).

Leave it—Don't touch it. Preferred over the use of "No."

Let's go—Used to get dog's attention to follow you.

Load—Get into a vehicle or crate (also Load up).

Nein (German)— (*pronounced nine*) No (*see* No, Phooey).

No—Stop immediately. Reserved for use in emergency situations

threatening life or serious injury. This word is overused and will lose its effectiveness if used too much (*see* Nein, Phooey).

Off—1. Remove yourself from atop of where you are. 2. Used to have the dog stop jumping on you and other people.

OK—1. Approval of an action. 2. Release from a stationary position (*see* Free dog, Go play).

Out—1. Release from a confined area. 2. Remove yourself from an area.

Over—Jump over an object or barrier.

Paw—Shake hands or used to examine the feet (*see* Five).

Phooey—Used in place of No (*see* Nein).

Place—Go to a preselected place and stay there. This is used as an alternative to sleeping quarters.

Platz (German)— (*pronounced plots*) Down.

Play dead—Lie down on your side and do not move.

Quiet—Stop barking (*see* Shut up).

Recall—Calling your dog to come to you after being released to work.

Refind—Relocate the source in the same manner as "Show Me."

Roll over—Generally used as a trick but can be useful in examining your dog. This command is used to have the dog roll from one side to the other.

Search—Alternative to Seek (*see* Seek, Sook).

Seek—Begin looking for something (*see* Search, Sook).

Shake—1. Shake hands. 2. Shake off water on its coat, as in "Shake it off," "Shake it up" (*see* Five, Paw).

Show me—Take me to what you have found. If you are not in the area when the dog finds his prey, you may direct him by using this command to have him take you to the location.

Shut up—Used to cease barking or begging (*see* Quiet).

Sit—In an upright position with the rump on the ground.

Sits (German)— *(pronounced seats)* Sit.

Slow—Slow down when working or walking too fast (*see* Easy).

Sook—Alternative to Seek. Begin looking for something (*see* Search, Seek).

Speak—Used to extract a bark from the dog.

Stand—Stand upright on all fours.

Stay—Remain in the position placed *(see Bleib)*.

Stop—Cease what you are doing now (*see* Leave it).

Take it—Obtain possession.

Too far—You have gone beyond the prescribed limit of work and must return.

Toy—Name given to the dog's reward.

Treat—Same as for Cookie (*see* Cookie).

Truck—1. Used to have the dog board the back of a pickup truck (*see* Load). 2. May also be used for homing (*see* Home).

Under—Crawl beneath, as opposed to going over.

Up or Hup—Get upon or over an object or structure.

Visit—Go to another person (*see* Go to).

Wait—Pause or stop your motion until released.

Work—A prescribed activity other than play. Used to get the dog's attention. Generally used as a question.

Yard—Report to a prescribed area other than living quarters, crate, house or kennel (*see* Crate, House, Kennel).

Toxic Substances

Below is a list of common household products that are toxic to dogs. These are common substances that most people have in their homes. If by chance your pet ingests any of the following, call the vet immediately. This is what to look for and how to initially treat your dog for poisoning until you get further instructions from a veterinarian.

Ammonia
Signs: Vomiting blood, abdominal pain, skin blisters, and burns.
Treatment: Wash skin with water and vinegar, give water mixed with small amount of vinegar, or you may give three egg whites orally.

Antifreeze
Signs: Vomiting, coma, kidney failure, death.
Treatment: Further induce vomiting, then administer one ounce of vodka orally followed by water.

Bleach
Signs: Burns of skin and mouth, vomiting.
Treatment: Further induce vomiting, give three egg whites orally.

Charcoal lighter fluid
Signs: Vomiting, breathing distress, shock, coma, or seizures.
Treatment: Further induce vomiting.

Detergents/Soap
Signs: Vomiting.
Treatment: Further induce vomiting, give three egg whites or milk orally, watch breathing.

Furniture polish
Signs: Vomiting, breathing distress, shock, coma, or seizures.
Treatments: Further induce vomiting, give laxatives.

Gasoline
Signs: Skin irritation, weakness, dementia, dilated pupils, vomiting, twitching.
Treatment: Further induce vomiting, give vegetable oil orally to block absorption, get into fresh air.

Ibuprofen
Signs: Vomiting, stomach ulceration, kidney failure.
Treatment: Further induce vomiting, give laxatives.

Insecticides
Signs: Excessive drooling, weakness, seizures, vomiting, dilated pupils.
Treatment: Wash off insecticide, administer atropine sulfate as the antidote.

Kerosene
Signs: Vomiting, breathing distress, shock, coma, or seizures.
Treatment: Further induce vomiting, give laxatives, give vegetable oil orally to block absorption.

Paint thinner
Signs: Vomiting, breathing distress, shock, coma, or seizures.
Treatment: Further induce vomiting, give laxatives.

Rat poison
Signs: Excess bleeding, anemia, cyanosis.
Treatment: Induce vomiting; requires vitamin K injections.

Rubbing alcohol
Signs: Weakness, lack of coordination, blindness, coma, dilated pupils, vomiting, and diarrhea.
Treatment: Further induce vomiting; give baking soda in water to neutralize acidosis.

Turpentine
Signs: Vomiting, diarrhea, bloody urine, neurological disorientation, coma, breathing distress.
Treatment: Further induce vomiting, give vegetable oil by mouth to block absorption, give laxatives.

Tylenol
Signs: Depression, fast heart rate, brown urine, anemia.
Treatment: Induce vomiting; give 500 mg vitamin C per twenty-five pounds of dog weight, followed by baking soda in water.

Note: How to Induce Vomiting
Give several teaspoons (for small and medium dogs) or several tablespoons (for large and giant dogs) of hydrogen peroxide orally. Repeat as needed to stimulate vomiting.

Another remedy: Use one teaspoon (for small and medium dogs) or one tablespoon (for large and giant dogs) of syrup of ipecac. Allow the dog to drink one cup of water, as this will hasten the vomiting. Repeat as needed.

Acknowledgments

This book would not have been possible without the generous contributions of individuals willing to share their thoughts, knowledge, and experiences. Thanks to these individuals, we are able to train dogs to the best of their abilities. With sincere appreciation of their works, I thank and reference the following:

Books:
American Rescue Dog Association, *Search and Rescue Dogs* (Howell House)
Sandy Bryson, *Search Dog Training* (Boxwood)
Hatch Graham, *Scent Behavior and Training Notes*
J.A. Kersley, *Training the Retriever* (Howell House)
Milo Pearsall and Hugo Verbruggen, *Scent* (Alpine)
William Syrotuck, *Scent and the Scenting Dog* (Arner)
Cpl. Robert G. Teather, C.V. Royal Canadian Mounted Police, *Encyclopedia of Underwater Investigations* (Best Publishing)
Leon Whitney, *Dog Psychology* (Howell House)
Malcolm Willis, *Genetics of the Dog* (Howell House)

Training Notes and Seminars:
Bill Tolhurst, Marian Hardy, Brook Holt, Andy Rebmann

Law Enforcement Training Specialists, Phase I-IV, National Narcotics Detector Dog Association— Billy Smith, Carol Baronni, Eddie Rodrigue, Larry Crum, Phillip Goodwin
Mass Fatalities Incident Response Course, Emergency Management Institute, National Emergency Training Center
Medicocriminal Entomology, American Board of Forensic Entomology
Mary Menhein, Director, Forensic Anthropology, Louisiana State University, Baton Rouge, LA
Crime Scene Investigations— Capt. Ronnie Frey, St. Tammany Parish Sheriff's Office, Covington, LA

Personal Instruction and Training by:
Mike Strain, DVM, Claiborne Hill Veterinary Hospital, Covington, LA

Susan Strain, DVM, Claiborne Hill Veterinary Hospital, Covington, LA
Tommi Pugh, DVM, Claiborne Hill Veterinary Hospital, Covington, LA
James Hendry, DVM, General Animal Hospital, Covington, LA
Greg Lebranche, DVM, General Animal Hospital, Covington, LA
George Strain, DD/V/M, PhD, MS, Director Veterinary Medicine, Louisiana State University, Baton Rouge, LA
Lawrence Myers, DVM, PhD, MS, Director Veterinary Medicine, Auburn University, Auburn, AL
Cpl. Robert G. Teather, Public Service Diver, Royal Canadian Mounted Police, Delta, BC, Canada

About the Author

- Master Trainer in obedience, tracking, hunting, search-and-rescue, and detector dogs since 1980.
- Court-certified in 1998 as an expert in the field of canine training and tracking through the Criminal District Courts of New Orleans, Louisiana.
- United Kennel Club (UKC) all-breed conformation and Junior Showmanship judge.
- American Kennel Club Canine Good Citizen evaluator.
- Licensed in 1992 by the Drug Enforcement Agency as a researcher in the field of canine training.
- Studied and trained in canine psychology, animal behavior, breeding and genetics, and canine nutrition and health care.
- Trained and experienced in handling dangerous, vicious, and nuisance animals since 1994, with a commendation from St. Tammany Parish Sheriff's Office, Louisiana.
- Founding member and trainer of Louisiana Search and Rescue Dogs, Inc. (LASAR), 1989–1996.
- Member of the National Association of Search and Rescue (NASAR), 1989–2000.
- Retired Lieutenant with St. Tammany Parish Sheriff's Office, Louisiana, Search and Rescue Division.
- Owner, handler, and trainer of Ladyhawke, the first registered Louisiana Catahoula Leopard Dog certified in Search and Rescue and Narcotics Detection to be commissioned by law enforcement and receive the Service Champion Award for outstanding work in community service. Presented by the National Association of Louisiana Catahoulas (NALC).
- Recipient of the Excellence in Training award presented by Sigma Chemical Corporation.
- Author of *Louisiana Catahoula Leopard Dog*, a book on the history, breeding, and care of Louisiana Catahoulas.
- Member of the Association of Pet Dog Trainers (APDT).
- Certified breeder of registered Louisiana Catahoula Leopard Dogs since 1985 (NALC).
- Past president of the American Catahoula Association.
- President of the Catahoula Owners, Breeders, and Research Association (COBRA), a UKC single-breed organization.
- Vice president of the Great Southern Kennel Club, a UKC multi-breed organization.

Index

CPSIA information can be obtained at www.ICGtesting.com
Printed in the USA
BVOW11s0958060215

386698BV00003B/3/P